97

Savvy Secrets
for Protecting
Self and School

To my wonderful husband, Frank

97
Savvy Secrets for Protecting Self and School

A Practical Guide for Today's Teachers and Administrators

Alice Healy Sesno

CORWIN PRESS, INC.
A Sage Publications Company
Thousand Oaks, California

For information:

Corwin Press, Inc.
A Sage Publications Company
2455 Teller Road
Thousand Oaks, California 91320
E-mail: order@corwinpress.com

SAGE Publications Ltd.
6 Bonhill Street
London EC2A 4PU
United Kingdom

SAGE Publications India Pvt. Ltd.
M-32 Market
Greater Kailash I
New Delhi 110 048 India

Printed in the United States of America

Library of Congress Cataloging-in-Publication Data

Sesno, Alice Healy.
    97 savvy secrets for protecting self and school : a practical guide for today's teachers and administrators / by Alice Healy Sesno.
        p. cm.
    Includes bibliographical references.
    ISBN 0-8039-6728-4 (cloth: acid-free paper). —ISBN 0-8039-6729-2 (pbk.: acid-free paper)
        1. Teachers—Conduct of life. 2. Teachers—Professional ethics.
    3. Teacher-student relationships. 4. Classroom management.
    5. Teaching—Vocational guidance. 6. School administrators.
    7. Schools—Security measures. I. Title. II. Title: Ninty-seven savvy secrets for protecting self and school.
    LB1775.S46 1998
    371.1—dc21   97-45461

This book is printed on acid-free paper.
98 99 00 01 02 03 10 9 8 7 6 5 4 3 2 1

Production Editor: Sherrise M. Purdum
Production Assistant: Lynn Miyata
Editorial Assistant: Kristen L. Gibson
Cover Designer: Marcia M. Rosenburg
Print Buyer: Anna Chin

Contents

ల౷ర౷ు

SAVVY SECRET NUMBER	
13	Let no child leave during school hours without signed permission. (See Savvy Secret #35, too.)
14	Never keep a suicide threat a secret. (See Savvy Secret #49, too.)
15	Beware the power of the press, radio, TV, and the Internet.
16	Always inform parents of curriculum changes.
17	Don't give medical advice to students.
18	Don't give medication to students.
19	Don't take school records out of the building.
20	Never release a student to a stranger without a custody order.
21	Don't release records to strangers.
22	Never talk about students in a negative manner.
23	Report *all* accidents, even if no visible harm or injury results.
24	Never put a student out of class.
25	Inform administration *immediately* of unauthorized student exits.
26	Always salute the flag.
27	Don't laugh or talk at those special times.
28	Don't show films or videos you haven't seen.
29	Check out the holidays and their symbols.
30	Watch the time.
31	Dress appropriately.
32	Don't bring personal belongings or issues to school.
33	Don't search students or their possessions.
34	Don't assign potentially dangerous homework.
35	Never allow a sick child to go home alone.

Preface

❧❦❧

G ood educators are a rare and dedicated group. Perhaps they are not yet an endangered species. But, like an endangered species, they should be nurtured and valued because of their value to our society and civilization.

Too often, educational environments can become incompatible with the goals of education, and teachers can be prevented from giving their gifts of learning and compassion by a frightening matrix of competing social and professional agendas. Every teacher can tell horror stories about colleagues whose careers have been ruined because of innocent missteps in efforts to fulfill their *perceived* obligations as teachers.

The goal of this book, *97 Savvy Secrets for Protecting Self and School*, is to make the path a little clearer, to identify the pitfalls and missteps that can be predicted and avoided. It was written out of concern for dedicated educators and with the hope that readers will persevere in their mission of providing students with the social and academic building blocks they need for satisfying and constructive lives.

To do this, teachers and administrators *must* safeguard themselves; arm themselves with self-protecting knowledge; and, in some instances, reprogram themselves with new behaviors, new responses to their perceptions of students' needs. Unfortunately, the helping reflex that so many of us bring to the profession must be replaced with alternative responses—and the discipline to use the guidance provided in this book.

Education seems to have become a game of political compromise in some districts, with teachers having to implement public policies that have little to do with reading, writing, and 'rithmatic. Teachers must confront issues—and manage classrooms—in ways that were unimaginable several decades ago.

Along the way, classroom teachers have become ever more vulnerable to allegations of misconduct or malfeasance—because there are more legal and procedural booby traps to trip the unwary. And as every teacher knows, once a teacher is accused of *anything*, however falsely or maliciously, a career stain results that may never be removed.

In the process, administrators, too, can sustain career damage if they attempt to defend classroom teachers or to propose penalties less severe than those being argued for at more senior (political) levels or advocated by parents or community groups. (Some allege that administrators abandon teachers who get into trouble. Perhaps that happens in a few cases, but most often, administrators are as powerless to prevent career damage to teachers as are the teachers themselves.)

Meanwhile, teacher preparation continues to be focused on content and methodology—necessary, but not sufficient for career survival.

That's why this book had to be written. That's why survival rules are needed that point out hidden dangers and provide cautionary notes that steer you away from career-killing episodes.

Ours still is a wonder-full profession, with ample opportunities for making major differences in the lives you touch. But when a teacher stumbles, children suffer. Children never win when teachers lose control of classrooms, lose the support of administrators, or lose in contests with parents and special-interest groups.

Read these *97 Savvy Secrets*, discuss them with your colleagues, and refer to them frequently by flipping through this book in 30-second or 2-minute "refresher reviews." Then, forewarned and forearmed, you can focus on teaching, contributing, and loving your chosen work and your students.

Acknowledgments

Much thanks to the many educators who shared their stories and expertise with the author—especially

Clara Blumenthal, Lana Brody, Dr. Gordon Footman, Carol Fox, Dr. Alan Hoffman, Dr. B. J. Korenstein, Ronald J. Rhodes, Lynn Sabin, Grace Smilde, Lily Wilson, and the very helpful Gerri Jordan.

Very special thanks to Dr. Woodrow Sears—idea man, motivator, and editorial sage.

About the Author

Alice Healy Sesno was a teacher in the New York City school system and an administrator with the New York State Education Department and the Los Angeles County Office of Education. She has served as the Director of the Illinois Project for Law Focused Education and on the faculties of Fordham University in New York City and Loyola University in Los Angeles. She has guest lectured at universities across the United States. She resides at present in Palos Verdes, California, with her husband, Frank.

Never leave your class alone!

You have been given the responsibility of a classroom full of students. You are to act in loco parentis, in the place of parents, and to be the responsible adult in all classroom situations. If you step out of the room momentarily, regardless of reason, your responsibility remains behind in the classroom. Telling the teacher next door or across the hall that you are leaving does not absolve you of responsibility nor can another teacher assume your responsibilities without abrogating his or her obligations to another group of students. If you must leave your class, you must ensure that a *regularly authorized person* is in the room *before* you leave.

If you have a parent visiting, a school monitor, or a teaching intern assisting, do not assume that your liability for what happens in your classroom transfers to that other person. Check this out with your administrator or principal. Make certain you know the procedure for notifying the main office and getting coverage for your class *before* you have to make an emergency trip to the bathroom, need to make a phone call, or step outside to speak privately to a student. Teachers have been held liable for injuries sustained by students during an absence of a few minutes.

Why is this the #1 Savvy Secret? Because it is fundamental and because everyone has seen it violated. If you are going to protect yourself, this is where it begins. Expect the worst, and defend against it!

MOTTO: You're responsible, so be there!

Keep the door open when you are alone with a student.

Students need individual attention. Teachers should spend time with each student, one on one, to ensure that there is an opportunity to share information that might not come out in class. In some cases, that may be the only opportunity a student has for a *positive* conversation with an adult. But. . . . As media reports and movies point out, few things ignite public rage so much as when teachers and other adults are accused of violating the boundaries of appropriate relationships with young people they are chartered to serve. Few accusations are as difficult to defend against. *Do not put yourself in a compromising position.* Keep all dealings with students in front of open doors or windows or in the presence of responsible witnesses (who may be other students). Meeting with students off campus, particularly in a teacher's home (no matter how many others are present), is a questionable practice. Even on official field trips, avoid one-on-one involvement with students. While many people are on the playground, you may walk and talk with a student or sit on a bench. If there are counselors' offices with half-glass doors, perhaps you could arrange to use one for a one-on-one discussion. In all instances, look at your every contact with students through the eyes of the most suspicious persons you could imagine, and then, *give them nothing to imagine and gossip about.* Missteps here have created difficult times for teachers and destroyed many careers.

MOTTO: Use prudence when conferring with students.

Never hit a student!

This shouldn't require explanation, but it happens so often that something must override intelligent adult responses. The children put in your charge come with all kinds of backgrounds and some are disrespectful, mean, cruel, and violent. And for some, provoking adults to the point of physical abuse has been their only means of getting attention. Don't rise to the bait!

Also, there are antecedents in educational lore about hitting students with rulers, grabbing and shaking them, shoving them against the chalk board—all in the name of discipline. Aside from being a poor pedagogical technique (because who wants to model physical punishment as the path to learning?), it's very dangerous. An adult's blow in anger can maim or kill a child. An accumulation of blows (perhaps on top of those administered at home) can result in serious medical complications. At all costs, teachers must restrain themselves. Beyond the moral imperative not to become abusive with students is the absolute certainty that, if legal action is taken by parents, guardians, or advocates, the teacher could be found guilty and liable for punitive damages beyond loss of job and career.

Learning how to discipline children—how to get them to follow rules and examples of appropriate behavior—is one of teaching's most difficult skills. And the most difficult part of all is for teachers to learn to discipline themselves to recall sound educational techniques when their anger rises.

MOTTO: Hands are for healing, never for hurting.

Before you file a grievance, clear it with a union representative.

Teachers have rights, and they have representatives to be their advocates when their rights are violated. Disagreeable things, unfair things, dumb things can happen to make teachers as individuals and as a group feel demeaned, diminished in value, and just plain angry. Things that appear intentional may be, but you may not have grounds for a grievance.

Don't file until *you ask the union representative* to make sure that

- Your issue is covered by the contract
- Your presentation of the case is accurate
- You have explored other options for resolution or relief

It's your privilege to file a grievance, but it's possible that you will be resented by your principal, the school staff, and teachers too frightened to grieve. Collectively, they can create a lot of personal anguish for you. That's why you should *grieve your own issues* and not be pushed into filing by others who lack courage to speak for themselves. Those who encourage you may not stand with you at the hearing and may deny their complicity.

Although it's your right to file a grievance, think about it as a last resort to resolve issues such as class assignments, program schedules, class rotations, perceived favoritism, or other decisions that you think put you at a disadvantage. Sometimes, asking for clarification by the appropriate staff person may provide an acceptable explanation before you risk a grievance.

MOTTO: Try your interpersonal skills first; view grievances as a last resort.

Handle discipline yourself; things escalate when others intercede.

Discipline problems are tough—but they are the part of the job that defines your capabilities more than any other in the eyes of administrators and other teachers. Unless something *very* violent or dangerous is happening that could not be contained by any single professional, handle it yourself or risk being seen by administrators as at much at fault as the troublesome students.

Administrators are there for you, but rescuing teachers and calming out-of-control classrooms are not favorite activities. When those episodes occur, questions are raised about supervision and control that have potential for damaging the careers of all concerned. They cannot add to your stature as a promotable professional. In fact, quite the reverse is true.

But you are *not* alone in the classroom. Even first grade students can help with troublesome classmates; that's why there's been some form of buddy system or teaming in classrooms as long as anyone can remember. Even teenage students will support classroom behavioral requirements that they understand and take part in creating. It's called *participative management* in industry. You could call it *participatory citizenship* and allow students to help set boundaries needed for classroom activities and learning, with rewards for everyone when rules are maintained. When they aren't, what do students think are appropriate sanctions? Everyone wins when classrooms are effective learning environments—and everyone learns.

**MOTTO: Create a classroom "family"
that solves its own problems.**

Make sure your school's policies concur with state policies.

This is a heavy burden to put on teachers, but sometimes, school districts—and even schools—are governed by rules developed as conveniences by administrators. Sometimes, local policies and procedures are not congruent with state demands. In these increasingly confusing and litigious times, teachers must be aware of the protocol they must follow to be held blameless should litigation follow. Specifically, when child abuse is discovered or suspected, many jurisdictions require that the child care provider (teacher) accept responsibility for reporting such information to the legally constituted authorities (e.g., local police, sheriff, or Department of Children's Services). Only one of these agencies may be the specified recipient of the information; and although the law may allow others than the teacher to make official notification, the teacher *cannot* be absolved of responsibility by passing the information to a counselor or administrator. Here is the bottom line: If you discover evidence of child abuse, it may be necessary but it is *not* sufficient to tell your principal. You must ensure that the information is reported as required, or you can be held liable.

Recommendation: Make the call yourself from the principal's office or be with the principal to hear him or her make the call, and *log the date and time on your calendar; use the school's date-time stamp to validate your entry.* This is one of the times when you *must* know and follow *state* rules.

MOTTO: Ignorance of the law is no excuse; cover your actions.

Always keep a copy!
(Especially of child abuse reports!)

There is no substitute for a paper trail, records that indicate school policies were observed by a person who keeps records. Educational administrators are no different from professionals in other fields in this regard: They respect and respond to documentation. Where there is no documentation, issues get resolved on the basis of reputation and hierarchical position. When decisions are made that way, teachers are put at risk unnecessarily.

Make a photocopy of all reports submitted for official purposes. If available, use the school's time-date stamp to validate yours as a true copy. If *child abuse* is involved, make certain you have a copy of the official report with dates, times, witnesses, anecdotal information, agency notified, person(s) contacted, and other actions taken. For *accidents or other incidents*, keep copies of reports filed, including names, date and time, precipitating factors, witnesses, and actions taken at the time; also record names of people you interviewed or who interviewed you and, in summary, what you were told or what you said (people have been misquoted).

Keep copies, too, of any notices to

- Ꮿ Dismiss class earlier than usual
- Ꮿ Change the official name of a student
- Ꮿ Anything regarding disciplinary actions against a student or yourself

Paranoid? Good records prevent bad outcomes for good people!

MOTTO: Good records are a teacher's best friend!

Take restrained children to the school nurse immediately.

If you physically intervene to break up a fight or for any other reason have to hold or restrain a student, take the child to the school nurse immediately. The nurse can determine whether injuries have been sustained by the student that could have been inflicted by your restraint measures.

The story is told of an East Coast teacher who grabbed and held an angry child who threatened to "off" a classmate who had made disrespectful remarks. Neither child struck a blow, but the child restrained by the teacher was so enraged by the restraint that he intentionally bruised himself and accused the teacher of manhandling him. A doctor confirmed the presence of deep bruises, and the parents threatened to sue the teacher and the school. Fortunately, the child confessed his self-inflicted bruises.

If a child becomes so angry that physical restraint is needed, a visit to the school nurse for a cool-down period is indicated. If there is no nurse on site to provide a physical inspection, call the principal, other faculty, or responsible students to witness the student's condition and attitude. Furthermore, it is good practice to get the names of witnesses to the original episode and restraint procedures who can, if needed, testify that the restraint was necessary for the safety of the students involved.

Students of all ages are under great pressure and, with daily doses of TV violence, conflict resolution in schools can become increasing physical.

MOTTO: Check the holding so it doesn't hold you back.

Keep five super lesson plans in reserve for desperate moments.

If your school gets an unexpected visit from the district super-intendent and your class is selected for the VIP visitor, you must be able to present a sparkling example of classroom deco-rum, excited learners, and appropriate visual aids. Likewise, if you must accept a temporary assignment with a class of "special attitude" students, you need to have an entertaining package of materials to survive the day.

There will be challenging days when a student is killed on the way to school, a student's parent dies, some local disaster occurs, or something else happens that breaks the classroom routine and attention of students. Media reports have shown how crisis counselors converge on schools when a tragedy occurs, offering assistance to students to deal with grief. Should that happen in your school, you *know* your usual lesson plans won't work.

Remember, special lesson plans often need special equip-ment. Make sure everything you need is available, including a spare bulb for the overhead projector (if it's used) so you can "show and tell" with confidence and ease. Don't be like the teacher whose emergency science unit required a bunch of car-rots. Her roommate made an emergency delivery but, when the carrots were tossed over the divider, they landed on the head of the visiting state assistant superintendent! Some drivers keep emergency kits in their cars for earthquakes or snow. Keep your emergency lesson plans close at hand.

MOTTO: Be prepared to sparkle in emergency "show and tell" situations.

Build rapport with your classes.

A favorite question to teachers is, "Would you like to be a student in this class?" Some decline to answer. Others say, "I'd like to be a kid again," but that's not the same thing. Others say, "Not with these kids." What comes through too often is that many teachers do not like their students!

Teaching cannot become "just a job." That attitude is as transparent as overt racism. Students often live horrendous home lives, and frightening encounters on the streets are routine. Many have no models of positive living other than the adults they encounter at school. When they discern that their teachers do not care about them—and they will pick that up faster than a dollar bill found on the street—they have no option than to treat teachers as they do other adults: with distance, distrust, and disdain.

Students should be *your* advocates, should support you because they know that you support them. Students—children— become realists early in life. They know you cannot change the world they come from each morning and return to each afternoon. What they need is your unqualified acceptance, your attention to them while they are in your care. Your care often is the only stable relationship they know, and we cannot know how vital that is in the decisions they make to become citizens or outcasts.

Teachers who "win" with students are protected in a way. The students say things to others, such as "She's okay. Don't give her trouble." High accolades!

**MOTTO: Be there for your students,
and they will be there for you.**

Put your best foot forward on Open School Night.

⋐⊙⊙⊇

The name of the game is teamwork and partnership. Never is that more important than on Open School Night. There are two major groups of parents to be concerned about: first, the parents who attend and second, those who don't. For both groups, preparations are necessary.

Parents who attend will appreciate the businesslike preparations of teachers who have folders readily available so their students' work and the teacher's observations can be reviewed. It gives parents confidence that their children are in the hands of a professional. Neatness is important, too.

Some schools require teachers to present to parents a lesson similar to the one their children will receive. Make it sparkle! In addition,

- ⤇ Know each student's name and *correct pronunciation.*
- ⤇ Make a schedule for the evening that lets all parents get equal time with you and to ensure that none monopolize your time.
- ⤇ Make your room as presentable and attractive as possible.
- ⤇ Have something positive (and accurate!) to say about each student.
- ⤇ Create a list of books, videos, museums, and other learning resources that parents can access to support their children's education.
- ⤇ If school policy permits, offer parents the opportunity to make an audiotape of your conversation with them about their child.
- ⤇ When you were a student, what did you want *your* parents to hear?

⋐⊙⊙⊇
MOTTO: Be prepared!
Make parents feel you and they are a team.

Form parent and student support groups to be your advocates.

In the same way that administrators respond positively to documentation, they respond positively when coalitions of parents and students petition in support of programs and teachers. Given the public's apathy, administrators pay attention when parents and students make coherent presentations in board meetings or other public forums. Teachers who are backed by parents and students tend to be treated deferentially by administrators.

In one school district, a new superintendent decided to economize by eliminating a group of student support personnel. On the posted date of the Board of Education budget hearing, the educators involved appeared to protest, but no parents or students appeared. The superintendent prevailed. In a similar scenario in a nearby district, 20 parents and 25 students showed up at the Board hearing to support the threatened service. It was not cut.

In the latter case, each service provider had formed "advisory" groups of five students and five parents. Groups met monthly for an hour over cookies and soft drinks to discuss programs and progress, review new research pertaining to the service, and to share concerns and questions. These meetings allowed parents and students to become invested in specific programs—and the programs' success. Involved parents won't allow "their" programs to be cut uncontested—or allow "their" teachers to be abruptly dismissed. But teachers must initiate and invite parent participation.

MOTTO: Don't go it alone— form student/parent advisory groups.

Let no child leave during school hours without signed permission.

School attendance is mandated by law. School buildings must conform to safety codes that guarantee safe learning environments. Teacher-student relationships are expected to conform to community norms and legal restrictions. Do not allow a child to leave that environment or change the explicit student-teacher relationship *without prior written approval of a parent or guardian.* This is nonnegotiable! Don't take chances!

Verbal permission is useless. If there is no written record, there is no defense. Somewhat better is the signed blanket permission that allows teachers and the school to send or take children off school premises during the school day. Blanket permission slips are administratively simple but legally inadequate if a parent discovers students are being exposed to subject matter content or hazards not anticipated at the time slips were signed.

Trips to museums, factories, historic sites, or school-sponsored academic or athletic events come to mind. But what about sending a trusted student out for your lunch or on a personal errand? Or to drive another student home or to a doctor? Did parents intend to approve these kinds of extracurricular activities? Does the school's liability insurance cover students engaged in these activities? Do they violate parents' rights to know where their children are at all times?

Other aspects of this savvy secret will be covered in #35.

MOTTO: Do only what's explicitly permitted; all else is prohibited!

Never keep a suicide threat a secret.

I'm going to hang myself in the garage some day soon so my body will be the first thing my father sees when he comes home with his new girlfriend. But be my only friend and don't tell anyone!

This young person is asking you to keep the secret of his or her life.

There can be no secrets where student welfare is involved or threatened. As the state-appointed guardian of students during the school day, you must not withhold any information that relates to student health or welfare. Consequently, if a student says, "I'm going to tell you something, but you must keep it a secret," *pay attention.* Usually, you will hear some kind of juvenile or adolescent dramatics, but if you hear about pills or drugs or razor blades, stop! Tell the student *immediately* that you cannot keep such a secret, that you are concerned, that you *care.* Be honest about being frightened for the child, scared that you cannot provide adequate support, and that you must get help for both of you. Don't delay!

You may hear students talking about a friend's suicide threat. Take it seriously. Inform your principal or school nurse; inform the parents; act to protect the student. For each child who succeeds in suicide, dozens of others fail but create avoidable injuries and heartbreak. Recent texts and curricula cover this vital area of student health and welfare. Teachers must make certain *they* are informed. Other "secrets" are covered in #49.

MOTTO: Keep a secret—put a student at risk.

Beware the power of the press, radio, TV, and the Internet.

Decades ago, children were told, "Fools' words, like their faces, often are seen in public places." That advice is apt today, with media representatives swarming around any type of incident or scandal looking for anyone who will speak, however few facts or qualifications they may have. In those instances, it's prudent to point media reps to administrators or designated spokespersons. You don't have to talk to the press. You put a lot at risk by doing so. If cornered, you can say, "I prefer not to discuss this now," or "You need to speak with someone who has all the facts." But if you choose to speak to the press, here are some guidelines:

- Don't speak negatively about students, staff, or others.
- Don't speak "off the record," because you may be betrayed.
- Report only what you *know* is factual—don't speculate.
- Act professional, using appropriate language and gestures.
- Inform school officials immediately—don't let them be surprised.

Once you are captured on video or audiotape, you have no control over how your words and meaning will be edited. Reporters and editors may not understand the situation or the context, and you may be misquoted. However, if you do something worthy of *positive* press attention, it's good politics to notify your school district *before* giving interviews. You may get useful support and allow the district to get a public relations boost in the process.

MOTTO: Don't trade 15 seconds in the spotlight for 15 years of torment.

Always inform parents of curriculum changes.

School curricula and community expectations can conflict. Advocacy groups may object strenuously to specific subjects or content that schools, in response to frightening social statistics, are addressing. Schools have become de facto socializing institutions at fundamental levels: gender identity, value clarification, dating skills, sexual harassment, self-esteem, suicide prevention, and even parenting skills. Not everyone agrees that schools should present nonacademic materials, and some parents choose to have their children excused from some classes. These issues should be resolved in advance by giving parents a program preview *after* it has been approved by your principal or district staff. That can be accomplished if teachers send students home with a letter of this type:

> Dear Parent,
>
> Our class begins a special 5-day program on suicide prevention in 2 weeks. It helps students identify suicide's warning signs and explains how to get help for others and themselves. The program was evaluated in California and praised. We expect it to help our students cope with the stresses of adolescence. If you have questions, please send a note and phone number so I may contact you. If I don't hear from you by (date), I'll assume you have no concerns about this program. Thanks for your interest and support.
>
> Sincerely,

Your thoughtful professionalism may prevent a firestorm of protest and allow your principal to resolve a problem quietly and constructively. Savvy Secret #65 speaks more fully to this point.

**MOTTO: Keep parents informed.
What they know can't hurt you.**

Don't give medical advice to students.

Four words parents don't want to hear: " . . . but my teacher said. . . ." That puts the parent and the teacher at odds, and that never should happen when health care is at issue. We've heard them all: Don't eat meat. Always sleep with the window open. Two aspirins always help me. Vitamin C prevents colds. That ankle is just sprained, so just rest and put ice on it (or heat). If you weren't so fat. . . . Just exercise. Just rest. You don't really need braces. It's probably just a wax buildup. You're just babying yourself. And so on.

Although it's useful to share personal anecdotes with students, make sure they don't constitute medical advice. You may not believe in using drugs; you may believe in the efficacy of herbal remedies; you may meditate daily or practice yoga; or you may be a practicing vegetarian. There's nothing wrong with any of that, so long as students don't quote you as an advocate. When students don't feel well, that's an opportunity to teach them how to seek proper help or remedies. They need to know how to research illnesses family members may have contracted and how to prepare for that important part of their lives: taking care of themselves physically and medically. But teachers can't point students in useful directions if they don't *listen and suspend judgment.* You can ask questions to help them clarify what they feel, but don't give advice! Remember, these are not adult peers. They are students. If you advise, you're asking for trouble!

MOTTO: An apple a day is just that!

Don't give medication to students.

Given Savvy Secret #17, it follows that you should *never* medicate a student, not even aspirin. If medication is to be administered, that's the role of the school nurse. However, teachers *may* oversee taking of prescription drugs at the *written request of the parent* and with permission of the principal.

In some instances, teachers may be asked by parents to remind students to take medications or, in others, actually to administer medications. If this makes you uncomfortable, ask the parent to make other arrangements. Medication, even in maintenance doses, is serious medicine. Explain your reluctance to participate so you don't communicate to the student any kind of disapproval that could reinforce in the student a desire to abandon the regimen. That could have serious consequences for you both.

If a student complains of stomachaches, dizziness, nausea, or cramps, *don't play doctor*. Respect your students; expect them to tell you the truth and refer them to the school nurse or administrator. Likewise, when they say they can't run during games or P.E., don't ridicule them. If you suspect that a student is malingering, find out why. Talk with the student, try to determine the underlying cause of his or her unwillingness to participate, call in a parent if necessary, and confer with your school nurse or counselor. One thing we know about behavior is that there always is an antecedent, a reason for the behavior you're observing. Look for it.

**MOTTO: Hesitate to medicate;
anticipate parents may litigate.**

Don't take school records out of the building.

School records are the school's products. Teachers come and go, students begin and finish, records remain. When students transfer, records must be sent to the new school so the unknown student has an instant history. And years after anyone would think it would matter, schools get visits from people in business suits doing background checks for sensitive government jobs. Naturally, they want to see the records of some long-gone student.

The advent of computers may mean that record loss will be less likely and record retrieval will be easier. Until that happens, teachers risk official rebukes by misplacing or losing records taken outside the school building.

One teacher took her records home in June to complete them before the end of the month. She stopped to shop for groceries. After dinner, she looked for the records. Detailed searches at home and school, plus several trips to the market, were fruitless. Six months later, she found the records safely preserved—in her freezer! Meanwhile, she received an official letter of reprimand that will be a permanent stain on her career, along with sustaining all the attendant embarrassment and loss of face.

Records management usually is governed by district policies, supported by school-specific procedures. Many school offices include a desk or countertop teachers can use to discourage them from removing records. Check your school's policy. Better, update records in the office.

MOTTO: Leave records where they belong.

Never release a student to a stranger without a custody order.

Custody of minor children is specified in divorce settlements, but there are various types of custody: sole, joint, divided (physical and legal). Teachers and schools must know each student's *custodial parent*. When custody changes, blanket permissions signed early in the school year may be invalid. Therefore, a copy of the custody order should be on file in the school office so teachers and administrators know whose signature is needed to authorize release of the student to people beyond school faculty and staff and with whom student records or performance may be discussed. If you are aware of divorce or hearings involving a child's parents, make sure you know who is the *current* custodial parent. Given the number of parental kidnappings, any person to whom students are released must meet these three criteria:

1. Prior *written* approval of the custodial parent
2. Proper identification if the adult is not known by the teacher
3. The child wants to go with the adult

Custody issues are particularly important for special education students, because parents must approve individual education plans and changes. When joint custody is involved, you or an administrator may have to go to court to get clearance on the plan. Likewise, if a student splits time between parents and demonstrates marked differences in appearance, homework preparation, or other behaviors, you may have to notify the court.

MOTTO: A copy of the custody order, please.

Don't release records to strangers.

A student's records are privileged information. Health records, academic standing, behavior and attitude observations, attendance—none of this is public information. Referring back to Savvy Secret #20, divorces multiply the numbers of people who may request and have information about students. Most districts have comprehensive guidelines for records management and security. Teachers should be familiar with them because many people—custodial and noncustodial parents, legal guardians, stepparents, foster parents, doctors, psychiatrists, receiving schools, sending schools, and judges—can request information about students. In brief, custodial parents and eligible students (over 16 years old) may see records, but a staff member should be present to assist in interpreting the material. When others see records, reviews should be in the school office, *not* in your classroom. Other generic guidelines:

- Verify identification and authorization of record reviewers.
- Make specific appointments for records review.
- If the school office will be used, give office staff advance notice.
- Arrange for as much privacy as possible if records are to be discussed.
- Don't let records leave your room or the school office.
- Check district policies on copying records in whole or part.
- If there are copying charges or fees, let reviewers know in advance.
- Ensure that records are returned in good order.

MOTTO: Records are for authorized eyes only.

Never talk about students in a negative manner.

Your experiences with students must be reported in appropriate and neutral terms. You never know who will overhear your comments about a student or who will repeat what they heard you say. Even if you are discussing a student in a positive context, if you use a derogatory adjective or label, the context will not matter. This is a time to invoke a variant of the Golden Rule—speak of others the way you would like to hear others speak of you.

The teachers' lounge, faculty lunchroom, or Friday afternoon "refreshment" clubs are places to relax and be yourself—but do not drop your guard! Avoid talking about individual students unless you are saying something unambiguously positive. If you are questioned about an incident in which a student was involved and you feel you must respond, remember to use "appropriate" and "neutral" to filter your response. Please note: It seems to be an imperative of human nature to pass along a negative story, which is the essential element of gossip.

Imagine the consequences if parents learn that their children have been the grist for a teachers' gossip mill or that their children are being defamed by a *professional* teacher. Parents know that teachers may not be able to resist prejudging students with poor reputations, lowering their expectations of the students and of the students' achievements as well. Such verbal indiscretions are the grist for legal mills. Although parents *must* send their children to school, they do not have to tolerate gratuitous defamation by careless, thoughtless comments.

MOTTO: A "word to the wise" should be a kind word.

Report _all_ accidents, even if no visible harm or injury results.

A student is hit on the head in a playground accident; another cuts her knees tripping over steps; another is frightened and cries when a light fixture falls near her; several report their bus driver had a near miss with a truck; a student gets a paper cut; another gets a nosebleed after bumping into a closet door.

Which of these must the teacher report? What does common sense say?

Forget common sense. If it happens, report it! Concussions may not be diagnosed until hours later. Cuts, scrapes, and even paper cuts can get infected. Yes, immediate attention, alcohol swabs, Band-Aids, and kind words are useful (if a school nurse is not available), but there is a larger educational issue involved.

Accidents always have a cause, and reports (a) build a data base on the kinds of school accidents so preventive measures can be developed; (b) record what happened and how the teacher responded, in case involved students have special medical or physical conditions; (c) create a document to send home with the student; and (d) identify _attitudes_ that allow accidents to happen.

Accidents provide natural opportunities to teach students about the relationship between inattention and consequences. Show them the reports that must be completed. Let them fill out reports. Ask them how to reduce classroom and school yard accidents. Maintain a chart of classroom accidents, and reward students when they can create a downward trend or a month with no accidents. This could initiate a lifelong mind set for risk avoidance. What a gift!

MOTTO: Don't let it go when someone should know.

Never put a student out of class.

Scenario: She's hit another child, thrown papers and books in a tantrum, called you obscene things, and told you where to go. Her classmates are excited and becoming more agitated as the performance continues.

Scenario: He arrives late for class, slams the door, opens with a string of expletives, struts into the classroom wearing a prohibited hat, chewing gum, giving the high sign to his audience, and flops noisily into his desk.

Reflex response: Get out of my room!

Teachers must react quickly and in a fully professional manner to prevent loss of control of the classroom. That means (a) giving the class an in-seat assignment to refocus them on learning, (b) attending to the disruptive student directly, and (c) getting someone to escort the female student to the nurse's office (or to the principal) and the male student to the disciplinary vice principal. Then, when the disruptive student is removed, return to the lesson plan.

No matter how provocative the behavior, teachers must not summarily expel a student from the room without (a) a specific destination and (b) an escort who is a school staff member or (c) a pass and a reliable student escort. Unfortunately, many schools must serve students who should be in other facilities, and that often proves a hardship for other students and faculty. But even disruptive students are required to be in specific classrooms at specific times. If teachers expel students without the described a-b-c structure, the teacher becomes legally liable for any physical or property damage that results.

MOTTO: Maintain school rules—they're your survival tools.

Inform administration *immediately* of unauthorized student exits.

As a corollary of Savvy Secret #24, teachers are required to ensure that students remain in assigned spaces. In the event of a family or police emergency, administration must be able to reach a student immediately—that is, to find the student in the designated classroom, shop, or activity area. If the student is not where he or she is expected to be and the teacher hasn't issued a pass, the teacher is in trouble!

It's relatively simple when a student stalks or dashes out of class in a noisy gesture of defiance or rebellion; the teacher and other students see the unauthorized exit and it can be reported immediately. It's more difficult when a student slips away from a work group and leaves the room. If the teacher is involved with other students and members of the work group did not see the exit, no one knows where the absent student is or that he or she is absent until the end of the period and everyone returns to assigned seats. The buddy system works well in these cases.

Legally, for the protection of the teacher, the school, and the district, every student must be accounted for at all times. No student may leave a classroom or be in other areas of the school without specific, written permission. That's the law! It's not negotiable! And it's what parents expect.

These ground rules need to be spelled out in every class at the beginning of the school year and restated periodically to ensure that students know there are responsibilities and consequences that govern all movements of students during the school day. Their understanding may make the teacher's control job easier.

MOTTO: You are your students' keeper.

SAVVY SECRET #26:

Always salute the flag.

Many school districts require that the school day begin with a formal flag salute, including the Pledge of Allegiance. Check this out with your principal. Find out *exactly* what the school's policy—and that of the sitting board of education—requires. Conveying an attitude of disrespect for the flag, for the Pledge of Allegiance, or school policies concerning them can bring protests, even from citizens who haven't had a child in school for 50 years!

In one instance, a dedicated, competent elementary teacher had a difficult student management problem—the bright-but-disruptive child of a school board member. Unfortunately, the child understood the parent's political leverage—and used it to full advantage to maintain distance with the teacher and other students. Despite the teacher's best efforts, the child could not be integrated into the classroom. That led to decidedly unpleasant meetings with the parent and the principal and culminated in active resentment by the child and parent. Despite the teacher's tenure and reputation, the principal could not protect her against the single allegation the board member made—that her class was so tightly scheduled that she neglected to incorporate saluting the flag into the daily regimen. The board member flew the flag of patriotism, and the teacher received a reprimand! This true story makes this important point: Many citizens feel aggrieved that so many things have changed since they were kids; the flag is their common denominator between then and now. Don't ignore it—or them!

MOTTO: I pledge to pledge!

Don't laugh or talk at those special times.

This is a corollary of Savvy Secret #26 regarding flag etiquette. This rule might have been subtitled, "When in Rome, do as the Romans do." Following closely on the heels of saluting the flag and giving time for students to recite the Pledge of Allegiance is remembering to stand and to place your right hand over your heart (left side of the sternum) when the National Anthem is played or sung. And for the sake of your career, don't laugh or joke about doing it, no matter how poorly it is sung.

As an extension of this, do not display disinterest in or disrespect for the rituals or children's activities in your school district or for any ceremonies conducted by clubs or lodges to which you might be invited. Participants in such activities believe in secret handshakes and otherworldly codes that may seem anachronistic to you. However, they are your *real* bosses and can cause you a great deal of grief if they suspect, by your behavior, that you are unappreciative of their passions. In local politics, one of them is likely to know a member of the board of education or someone in the superintendent's office, and the unwary teacher can become the center of a small uproar, totally unaware it was coming.

All of this, of course, has to do with image and the inescapable fact that teachers are role models. Most young people spend more time with their teachers than with their parents. Parents know this (but may not admit it) and become defensive when students exhibit behaviors that (a) they—parents—do not like and (b) were modeled by a teacher. Remember, "When in Rome . . . "

MOTTO: Be correct, circumspect, courteous, and compassionate.

Don't show films or videos you haven't seen.

With the advent or ready availability of VCRs in most classrooms, plus the wonderful library of educational videos being developed by foundations and commercial enterprises, many teachers have grown to rely on these rich and deep resources as supplemental (and sometimes, primary) instructional materials. (And how much easier it is to pop a video into the VCR than to fight with the bulky and often difficult 16-millimeter projectors of the recent past.)

At least three cautions need to be observed. One regards the copyrights on commercial videos and your district's policy about using them. Second refers to the broad area referred to as "age appropriate." And the third caution involves content that may be objectionable to some viewers—or to their parents. In an era of the mandated "V chip" and continuing debates about what children should be permitted to see, no teacher can afford to use teaching aids that will have parents calling or visiting the principal in protest or calling the local newspaper.

Use videos that carry all the appropriate seals of approval. Confer with your librarian. Ask your principal if there is a list of "not approved" videos.

Above all, do not show videos that have been brought in by students until you have reviewed them from beginning to end. There are videos that start like traditional movies or educational shorts but soon become displays of violence or sexuality clearly inappropriate for classroom use, regardless of age. There are thousands of approved videos available. Use them. Or preview very attentively!

MOTTO: The camera never blinks—so don't you.

Check out the holidays and their symbols.

Is Santa Claus a religious figure? Are Santas and reindeer, decorated cone-shaped trees, and even tree-shaped cookies going to be viewed as religious icons? Will children who don't receive fair shares of Valentine cards suffer diminished self-esteem? Check with your principal! Probably no school in the United States is without a policy on holiday decorations, their underlying religious messages, and prescribed means for incorporating conflicting beliefs and faith structures into the curriculum in a fair and balanced manner.

Schools, as public institutions, have been the battleground for religious and antireligious forces over several decades. The furor is unlikely to subside as the United States becomes increasingly multicultural and as so-called minor religions move into the mainstream. Remember, you can only lose, arguing about religion and politics. So don't allow those issues in your classroom to become lightning rods for the school and the school district. Check your district's policies *before* you decorate.

If policies are ambiguous, consider creating a decorating committee of students and parents (perhaps including an interior designer) to ensure that you are not standing alone if your decorations and classroom discussions are challenged. That way, style, color, and cost can become part of the learning, as well as sensitivity to the multicultural realities of the classroom and the school.

Using district guidelines or other teachers' resources, your classroom can become a conflict-free, ecumenical model that students will remember.

**MOTTO: Keep decorations
and discussions within district policies.**

Watch the time.

One of the first things taught in school is how to tell time. The school bell is remembered for summoning students to classroom discipline. Class bells mark the beginning and end of classes. For students who don't conform, tardy notes are a significant part of the school's paper flow. The lesson? Time matters!

Accordingly, teachers need to model time consciousness as well as other socially appropriate behaviors. That means arriving at school at or before the designated time, being in the classroom and prepared to commence the day's lessons when the class bell rings, and generally conveying to students that punctuality is an important part of adult responsibility. That means that classroom management should be precise so that students are not delayed in leaving one class en route to another. If there are a few slack moments, they belong to the students, and teachers should respect students' time as well as their own.

Likewise, teachers should be punctual when meeting with parents and ensure that meetings with students or parents do not conflict with meetings called by administrators. Being late to meetings and being hurried and unprepared are unprofessional behaviors. Some guidelines:

- ๑ Arrive at appointments with at least 5 minutes to spare.
- ๑ Anticipate traffic delays or other circumstances that could stall you.
- ๑ Create a system of time discipline that fits your needs and schedule.
- ๑ End meetings promptly; respect the time of those with whom you meet.

MOTTO: This is your time to make time work for you.

Dress appropriately.

It matters. In a study done with high school students, a lecture in an outdoor setting was presented by an instructor in casual attire. Similar content was presented in a classroom, though the instructor still was in casual attire. The third time, the same information was presented in a classroom, but the instructor was wearing a suit and tie. It was not surprising that students rated the most formal presentation as highest in importance and value.

Even on "casual Fridays," teachers must not allow their attire to create confusing images. "Who is the adult here?" should never have to be asked. Even on Halloween. Nor should skintight or otherwise revealing clothing *ever* be worn to school or to school-sponsored functions. Wearing sexually provocative clothes elsewhere is a matter of taste but could be a matter for censure in settings in which students or parents are present.

Being professional includes presenting oneself appropriately when on duty. In truth, teachers, as powerful role models, are off duty only in the privacy of their homes. A double standard? Professionalism requires it.

MOTTO: Remember, people still judge books by their covers.

Don't bring personal belongings or issues to school.

A classroom is no place for personal pictures or valuable gifts. One teacher discovered her prized porcelain cat had "walked" off her desk. It created an embarrassing episode for her, her students, and the principal. So don't bring personal items that will tempt students to steal or that you do not want to lose.

Another found himself being quizzed by administrators because of magazines brought to school to read on breaks or at lunch. Parents objected to the teacher's carelessness in exposing their children to adult-content material. How could this happen? Students saw, students talked, and concerned parents invoked their version of community standards.

Drugs, alcohol, and cigarettes have no place at school. Increasingly, entire campuses are declared smoke-free zones, so being seen with cigarettes in pocket or purse can lead to criticism. Any suspicion of drinking, doping, or being hungover on campus can bring prompt and painful encounters with administrators. Even being seen taking aspirin or prescription drugs makes a teacher subject to gossip and innuendo. If you must take medications at school, do it in the privacy of the rest room. Students do not need to be privy to your medical circumstances.

Justifiably, teachers feel ownership for "their" classrooms. It's natural to want to put a personal stamp on your working environment. But anything you bring into the classroom is subject to inspection and judgments by students and parents whose ideas about appropriateness may be very different from yours.

**MOTTO: A lot's at stake—be careful
what you take—to school or at school.**

Don't search students or their possessions.

Keep your hands off students. A welcoming handshake is professional, and an arm around a shoulder may be appropriate support for a grieving student. But that's about as far as it goes in the personal contact arena. Regardless of your motives, your behavior—your touching a student—is subject to misinterpretation.

Someone has taken a pen, pencil, money, candy, and so forth. You think you know which student took it. You stand the child up for a search, then you search the desk, and then the child's knapsack—and you fail to find the missing item. The student has been humiliated, and you can imagine how that story will be played and received that evening at home. If you fall into this trap, expect to have some unpleasant conversations in the principal's office. Then, there's the scenario in which conducting a "pat down" or frisking leads to allegations of improper touching or fondling. No one wants that grief! Or suppose the search is for a suspected weapon—and the student decides to use the weapon against you. Again, what does your school's policy permit or require? Perhaps yours is a school with a metal detector through which students must pass to keep guns and knives out of the school. Metal detectors usually come with sworn (armed) and trained personnel to make subsequent searches. Don't volunteer to help them. Conduct searches *only* after you have received clearance from your principal and have a copy of school district policy. Better yet, post that policy for your students to see and discuss it. Use it as a basis for talking about trust and responsibility.

**MOTTO: Search for the truth—
but don't search your students.**

Don't assign potentially dangerous homework.

Homework is an important and necessary extension of class-room work. But as in all other instructions teachers give students, screen your requirements for potential harm to your students. For example, a social studies teacher asked sixth-grade students to find and interview three homeless people—but did not provide guidance on supervision of this activity or by whom. Another teacher suggested students would understand better the mystery and poetry of a starry night by visiting a park at noon on Saturday and again after 10:00 Sunday evening. In both instances, parents were justifiably upset. In both instances, teachers and administrators were embarrassed by the poor head work.

Homework must be matched carefully to the age and intellectual ability of students; late-night assignments on a regular basis are not appropriate for 8-year-olds. Even assignments to visit a library can be an imposition on students in remote areas and without expected parental support. Cost also must be considered if homework requires visits to distant museums, use of expensive materials, or access to equipment or tools that may not be available in all homes. Computers are not yet in a majority of U.S. homes, and many students do not have access to one or to the Internet.

Teachers should be clear about the connection between classroom work and homework assignments, about desired outcomes that can be achieved by all students without undue hardship, extra expense, and personal hazard.

MOTTO: Align assignments with safe, achievable learning goals.

Never allow a sick child to go home alone.

"**I** live down the street, and my mother's at home." "I have a key and I always go home alone. I'll go straight to bed." Famous last words as feverish Betty trots out of your class to faint on the sidewalk or Jane with the splitting headache is abducted from the street by a passing stranger. These may sound melodramatic, but when such things happen, someone's career in education is over.

An ill child should go to the school nurse. If there is no nurse in your school, then the child should go to the principal's office. All schools should have a place in which students can rest with some comfort and privacy. A call to the parent or guardian can be made to determine the next steps (assuming the child isn't invigorated, if not healed, by a little tender loving care and attention). But these are decisions to be made by personnel in the principal's office, not the teacher.

Suppose the ill student is 16, one who drives and works part-time jobs and just wishes to rest at home. The procedure is the same: Someone in administration makes the decision and takes the responsibility (following district guidelines, of course). In the case of a student with continuing medical problems, signed parental permission in advance may be given to the teacher and to the principal to release the student as circumstances dictate—but even then, ensure that the student is escorted to either his or her home or that of a designated adult.

Teachers who are unsure (and older students can be powerfully persuasive) should not hesitate to have the student escorted to the nurse or principal.

MOTTO: When in doubt, don't let them out.

Ensure that parents understand what the consent slip permits.

All the consent slips are on file in the principal's office, and your field trip goes off without a hitch. The buses return from the science fair at 6 p.m. as scheduled, but you are met by frightened, weeping parents and TV cameras. The parents, recent immigrants, came to pick up their children at the usual dismissal time. Someone from administration tried to explain about the trip and the consent slips, but the parents (from a country where people disappear without cause) then thought they had signed their children away. This really happened!

Consent slips should be available in the languages parents speak. Teachers and schools cannot depend on child-parent communications to cover consent slips in English. Take the extra step to ensure that parents know what they are signing.

Likewise, if a student presents you with a parental note that requests what seems to be an unusual or unlikely degree of freedom, check it out. Students at surprisingly young ages can be clever forgers (sometimes with positive motives, like assisting an ailing parent or grandparent). If you can't reach the parent by phone or have difficulty communicating, consult your principal. Do not assume that the note (handwritten or typed) represents the parent's *actual* wishes.

To maintain the level of trust you hope to develop, tell the student why you're uneasy accepting the note and why you feel it necessary to speak with the parent or guardian directly. Explain, too, your liability if the wish of the parent or guardian has been misstated. Besides, what's a phone call among friends?

MOTTO: Communication & confirmation avoids consternation and confrontations.

Never condone bullying.

E veryone remembers a school-yard bully. Usually, it's a boy, but not always. But always, bullies are students having difficulties adjusting to school routines and discipline, changes or challenges at home, and behaving in socially acceptable ways. Schools exist, in part, to socialize students for success. That means teachers frequently must provide coaching for bullies and support for victims.

Several years ago, a student complained that he was being bullied; efforts by the teacher and administrators failed to stop the bully, so the student shot himself in front of the teacher and classmates. This tragedy makes two points: First, never tolerate bullying! Second, never discount a student's fear and distress.

When dealing with bullies, here are some strategies:

- ❦ Refer bullies for counseling, and involve parents in the solution.
- ❦ Be a role model for nonviolent responses.
- ❦ Use curriculum to highlight peacemaker roles.
- ❦ Help the school develop a policy regarding violence and intimidation.
- ❦ Build a teachers' library on handling bullies.
- ❦ Take courses on handling bullies and supporting victims.

When everyone's involved, bullies can be changed. Asking "Why do you pick on others?" rarely elicits a coherent response, because the bully's behavior is patterned, and he or she tends not to respond to logic. If parents, teachers, other school resources, and fellow students collaborate, bullies learn new ways to cope.

**MOTTO: Always listen with love—
early attention leads to prevention.**

SAVVY SECRET #38:

Grade up, not down.

Recent studies report that cheating is increasing while faculties are more reluctant to call students on it. This is a defeat for character-building and honor systems and demeans all grade-based criteria for promotion, schools' competitive standings, and college entrance. This is a major challenge for educators.

The national movement toward standardized achievement tests—and teaching children to pass them—probably will put more pressure on marginal students to cheat and on competent students to go along and get along. A partial remedy to this downward spiral is for teachers to *use grades to motivate students* and to make the grading system as clear as possible. Without throwing standards out the window, it's possible to work with kids, build their confidence, and in the process, reinforce (or teach them!) the joys of learning—and succeeding. Often, this means grading up instead of down when scores are close: a B– instead of C+.

In the scheme of things, is half of one point that important? Or even two points when you know the student has been pushing to improve and achieve? Isn't it likely that your vote of confidence will be repaid by continuing effort and results, because you are rewarding the behavior you want to see more of?

The "big picture"—equipping students to function effectively in an increasingly competitive world—is not served by scoring harshly. The benefit of the doubt is a vote *for* future effort, for nudging scores upward, for teaching kids that they can succeed, that cheating's unnecessary, after all. What a lesson!

MOTTO: Grade on the side of joy and success and excellence.

Don't give special gifts, and don't accept them.

Gift giving is troublesome. Your school probably has a policy regarding giving and receiving gifts. Read it and adhere to it.

If it's the custom in your school for teachers to give students gifts, here are some guidelines: (a) Gifts should be school related (pens, books, etc.). (b) Gifts should cost $2 or less. (c) Books should be from an approved list. (d) All boys should receive the same or similar gifts. (e) All girls should receive the same or similar gifts. (f) Don't give knives, candy, or other gifts that can inflict physical or dietary damage. (g) No student's gift should be larger, prettier, or more expensive than those received by other students or in any way convey the impression of a special relationship.

Before the December holiday season, communicate to students and parents (through a Classroom Procedures and Customs letter) that gifts to teachers are not allowed. If a student brings you a gift (a) thank the student warmly for the thought, (b) do not open the gift, (c) attach a note of appreciation and explanation to the parents, and (d) quietly ask the student to take it home, explaining again that you are following school policy. Be gentle to ensure that you do not embarrass the student. (If your school permits teachers to receive gifts, do not open gifts in the classroom; students may be embarrassed if their gift is smaller or less expensive than others; and any gift that is unduly expensive should be returned with a note of appreciation and explanation.)

All students are created equal, so don't let gifts interfere with that fact!

MOTTO: Beware of anyone bearing gifts.

SAVVY SECRET #40:

Allow no strangers in your classroom.

အလ္လ

A nyone who enters a classroom without proper identification and prior permission is there at the teacher's responsibility—and liability. Do not take this lightly.

She's there at the door, saying she's Tommy's sister and has brought his lunch bag. You've never seen her. If you allow her into the room, you're liable. If you accept the lunch bag, you sanction its (unknown) contents. If you let Tommy go out of the room, again you're liable. Therefore, your best option is to refer the woman to the office and let them handle her and the lunch bag.

Likewise, if you have parents or a special speaker coming to your room, ask them to stop by the school office to get a pass. This will prevent their being embarrassed by not being allowed into your room (or confronted by other school personnel in the hallways). It also gives your principal and office staff the opportunity to know who is in the building at all times. Without that knowledge, they cannot protect students and faculty from intruders and ensure that any unauthorized persons on the premises can be asked to leave or escorted out by police. Your principal and office staff will appreciate your cooperation, because without it, maintaining a secure school building is made more difficult.

Remember, this Savvy Secret and all others in this book are offered for *your protection* and for the protection of your students. If some seem unnecessarily restrictive, please think them through; if some seem too petty to merit your attention, please check them out with some of your more experienced colleagues.

MOTTO: Without a pass, you can't come to class.

Watch yourself at on-campus and off-campus parties.

Despite all that's been said for several generations about alcohol and schools, some people refuse to get the message. It's a rare high school dance at which there is no alcohol in hallways, smuggled into the building in raincoats or left in a locker earlier that day or a day before. Someone always wants to spike the punch with gin or vodka or both. Even teachers succumb to that mistaken idea of "fun."

In one instance, a male teacher made a pitcher of martinis to share with faculty friends to celebrate his coming wedding. He was overly jovial by the time parents and students arrived for his class's Christmas party. The hilarity and noise from his room suggested that some of the parents, too, drank from the silver pitcher. The principal arrived and was greeted effusively by the teacher and parents. Suspecting, but not wanting to discover, the principal withdrew to visit another room party. By some miracle, the parties ended, the teacher got safely home, and no complaints were filed. Today, no principal could afford to ignore signs of alcohol (or drugs). It's reckless beyond belief for a professional to endanger kids, the school's and principal's reputations, and his or her career for such unmistakable defiance of policy, practice, and common sense.

More than a few teaching careers have been tarnished by or surrendered to alcohol or drug abuse. Teachers seen imbibing at concerts, at ball games, or bars may discover there *is* a double standard—that some citizens demand that their teachers be role models in all public places as well as on school campuses.

MOTTO: Think before you drink! When liquor's there, beware!

Don't fail to report hazards.

Part of providing a safe learning environment is to ensure that the physical plant, too, is clean and safe from hazards. The custodians may not be as attentive as they should, and district maintenance personnel won't find every broken stair tread or exposed electrical wire. So if you see something out of order, report it.

In addition to reporting all accidents (see #23), it's necessary to report all broken or missing parts, window panes, floor tiles, stair treads, and so on. All of these can lead to injuries and to expenses that far exceed the cost of repairs. Usually, there's a form in the school office that teachers can use to report needed maintenance. Unfortunately, too many teachers complain about maintenance but don't bother to fill out the maintenance-needed form. If you haven't filed a form, you have nothing to follow up. If needed repairs aren't made, complain! If you see unsafe work practices (and students see them, too!), report them as well.

As always, there's a legal reason to report what you see. If you are aware of any defect or hazard in your classroom or on the campus and you do not report it, you can be held liable if a student—or another faculty member—is injured. The legal term is *contributory negligence.*

There are those on the faculty who routinely pick up candy wrappers and other trash on the campus; most don't. That's the custodian's job. But in terms of modelling good citizenship, showing students what it means to be a responsible adult, stoop to do things beneath your professional level. It pays dividends.

MOTTO: Don't let your neglect injure someone else.

Know your school's emergency plan (and have your own copy).

E very school should have an emergency preparedness hand-book. *GET IT!* Study it. Understand it. It may turn out to be the most important document you've read.

Usually, you will be asked to sign a receipt for the emergency preparedness booklet and perhaps to sign another document declaring that you have read it. Before you sign, make sure you have the material and that you've read it.

In the event of a fire, earthquake, or explosion, specific procedures are mapped for teachers to ensure the safety of students, specific exits to use, and specific assembly areas. To avoid confusion and delays in clearing the building or locating individual students or entire classes, follow procedures! Don't wait for fire drills to learn your routes and assembly areas. Don't fumble through fire drills and communicate to students that it's a dumb exercise. Don't fail to teach that emergency preparedness is a necessary part of being a responsible citizen, that only those who are prepared to cope and survive will be able to help others in emergencies, and that "what if" thinking can save the day. (Wouldn't it be wonderful if your students learned to locate fire exits in theaters?)

Teachers aren't asked to be heroes or heroines—just to be professional in their preparations to protect the children given into their care. That begins with *knowing emergency procedures in detail.* Then, when the fire bell rings, you can reflex into appropriate responses. Your certainty will be reassuring to students, and your disciplined response to the fire bell will model a powerful lesson.

MOTTO: Be prepared to land on your feet, not on your seat.

Don't detain students after school.

In the good old days (?), teachers could keep children after school as a disciplinary procedure, to have a quiet time to talk about classroom behavior or academic performance, or to give them a structured environment for completing missing homework. These days, this can be dangerous in at least three ways:

First, busing and carpooling parents create a demand for punctuality after school that was not common in the past. Missing the bus may subject a student to a long walk home or to a complicated series of changes on public transportation. Causing unaccompanied travel for younger students can bring teachers grief.

Second, delaying students can cause negative chain reactions. In one case, a student was allowed to drive to school. He was detained. His mother needed the car to go to work. She was detained. The principal received complaints from the employer, the parent, and the student. The teacher's status was diminished. Third, using after-school detention makes school a place of punishment instead of learning. Being permitted to stay after school should be a privilege.

In all instances, specific, dated, and signed parental permission should be in hand or on file before any student is allowed or required to stay in school past usual hours. Blanket permissions—"Keep Jane in from recess or after school anytime she misbehaves"—are not acceptable; neither is a student's statement that "My mother said I can stay late to decorate the gym." Obtaining parental permission a priori may seem unnecessarily bureaucratic. Do it anyway!

**MOTTO: Before keeping a child
after school, don't forget the consent-slip rule.**

Ensure safe use of all school equipment.

It's not only power saws and kilns in school shops that pose potential hazards to students but ordinary classroom "tools," such as pushpins, staplers, hammers, tacks, nails, scissors, and step stools. Increasingly, students arrive in school without life experiences teachers may expect, without digital dexterity, or without the physical agility or balance to stand on a chair without falling. Teachers should not assume students know how to use any tool safely. "Show and tell" prior to any student's first use of *any* school equipment. Usually, it just takes a minute.

Science materials and sports equipment—even helmets (which some kids will use to butt heads)—require careful demonstrations about use and warnings about abuse. Also, until you are comfortable that students are using equipment properly, *close supervision is suggested.* How do children drive staples through their fingers or nails through the pads of their index fingers or let boiling liquids splash in their eyes? Ask your school nurse. He or she can be an accident-prevention encyclopedia. (Also, be sure that all equipment is returned after use so school equipment is not involved in after-hours use or accidents.)

Again, parental consent is a good idea. A short note describing activities and equipment planned for the semester can be sent to parents, asking them to call or write if they have objections or questions regarding any item to be used. It takes only minutes to draft a memo and a minimum of administrative effort to let parents know you are working to include them as well as to protect their children.

MOTTO: Prevent the abuse of equipment use.

Keep the keys to your kingdom.

Any gear will disappear that's not under lock and key. Any records students can get to will be read and distributed. Perhaps there's no school in which at least one teacher does not have a purse pilfered or a wallet stolen each year—which then reminds everyone to keep their guard up and drawers and lockers locked.

Security works two ways. First, to keep "stuff" in and second, to keep people out. Regarding personal gear: If there's no place to lock it up, leave it home. Regarding school gear: Keep it in designated storage containers, and keep them locked. (Don't want to carry a lot of keys? Get multiple locks that open with the same key.) Create "key discipline," and build it into your routine. Many teachers use brightly colored wrist cords as key keepers; attaching a bell provides an auditory cue as well as a visual cue. Keep spare keys in the school office safe.

Don't let a student use your keys to go into a locked room on a personal errand or as a favor to you. That violates the school's security system. It also puts the student at risk—to be tempted to pry or steal or to be assaulted by an intruder in a locked and unsupervised space. Don't risk a crisis for inconvenience.

Your school will have security procedures, just as it will have emergency preparedness plans. Make certain you understand those procedures so you don't inadvertently set off alarms or compromise the school's system. Vandalism is a greater threat than physical harm, but you don't want to be the victim of either. Don't take shortcuts; don't take chances. Don't let your keys out of your control.

MOTTO: Ensure that you're secure—
follow the security plan *to the letter!*

When they've got to go—
they've got to go.

A delicate subject, perhaps, but a necessary one. Bowels and bladders do not always conform to 50-minute periods and other administrative schedules. Despite all other comments about hall passes and consent slips, when they've got to go, it's inhumane not to give permission. In fact, it's best if you can develop a relationship with students that permits them to leave the classroom when they feel it's imperative. Ideally, teachers should make their (and the school's) policy clear early in the semester and give students as much freedom as possible. Adults do not have to ask permission—they just leave. Can your students handle that?

Usually. However, if very young children (kindergarten through third grade) are involved, school policy may require that they be accompanied by an aide or a student buddy to protect the student as well as the teacher. It's possible to get children to confide that their stomachs are upset and that they may have to excuse themselves frequently. But when excessive toilet visits are observed, the teacher should inquire. Is the student ill? Is it the class subject matter, something that happened at home, or is it performance anxiety—reading aloud, taking a test, making a presentation in front of the class? Obviously, these are important issues for the teacher to uncover, in a gentle and sensitive manner. But because nothing in a classroom ever is *really* secret, it sends a message to other students that malingering or using toilet privileges to visit with buddies or to roam the halls is not okay. They will get the message and a major learning about freedom and responsibility.

**MOTTO: Teaching = moving students
to responsible adulthood. Start here.**

Question the questionnaire— don't collect data you don't need.

Classroom teachers are in an ideal position to mine data out of their classes to support theses or other graduate school research projects. Generally, students are pleased to participate, pleased to support a teacher who still is in the same relative place as they (i.e., sweating exams, grades, and graduation). Other teachers, too. With such an accessible population, there's a temptation to mine without permission. This Savvy Secret cautions against it and the possibility of data-collection errors.

Before using any research instrument in your school, *check school and district policies* (which may be restrictive). Ask your principal or another administrator to review your instrument and screen it for questions or areas of inquiry parents or others have challenged in the past. Questions about religious beliefs and practices, personal feelings about family and self, family composition and finances, and sexual activities or preferences generally are taboo. As personal privacy slips farther away, individuals and advocacy groups guard it ferociously.

Teachers are advised to notify parents through a note sent to the home that students may be asked to respond to a questionnaire to support graduate research projects. Parents should be told about content areas, given sample questions, and encouraged to ask for more information. Because a teacher's graduate studies are peripheral to the school's primary mission, parents may choose to not have their children participate in your research. That's their right, and it's *your* responsibility to avoid conflicts deriving from your research.

MOTTO: Take care when you pop the question.

Be careful when receiving any "secret" information.

eⱭⱭⱭⱭ

One of the hallmarks of really effective teachers is that students admire them, model behavior in their image, want to bond with them, and *confide* in them. That means that "secrets" come overtly or dribble into conversations, and teachers must be attentive to what they are hearing and careful about how they handle it.

Some secrets are the bubbles of adolescent excitement: "I'm going to ask Julie to the prom. Don't tell anyone." Some are moving: "I'm trying real hard for an A in math because it would surprise my dad. But don't tell anyone." Hearing these kinds of confessions is one of the joys of teaching.

But what if you hear secrets like these: "My uncle comes into my bed at night and does weird things to me. Please don't tell anyone." Or, "I'm going to get that Johnny for taking my girl. He'll be surprised when his brakes don't work as he speeds to her house. I hate him, and I'm going to get him. Please be on my side and don't tell anyone." All your skills will be needed to prevent a tragedy.

First, tell the student you can't keep such a secret, that you care too much about his or her welfare and pain. Make a case for the student's going with you to involve another professional—nurse, guidance counselor, principal—to get problem-solving help. Counselors and psychologists have some confidentiality privileges. Teachers don't. Where abuse is involved, teachers *must* report it (see Savvy Secret #7). Don't keep secrets that might cause harm to someone and make you and your school district culpable parties in posttragedy litigation.

MOTTO: Protecting the children is your first priority.

Don't change a grade on the record card.

One of the major reasons teachers are separated—fired!—is changing grades on the main record card. This book advocates giving students the benefit of the doubt, stretching points C+ to B–, from B+ to A–, to reward and motivate students who make visible efforts to improve their classroom performance (see Savvy Secret #38). This book cautions against changing grades once they have been posted. If a grade was entered in error, by the teacher or subsequently as a data entry error, schools have procedures for changing the original grade or test score. Ask for the procedure, and follow it! Usually, it will involve administration, parents, other teachers, and the student—a lot of people.

Why do teachers change grades? Sometimes, teachers succumb to pressures during a parental conference. Sometimes, they change grades from earlier in the year or a previous year to improve the student's grade point average at graduation. Sometimes, teachers discover that students cannot perform at levels predicted by earlier grades and decide to lower them—change them without authorization—to match current grades.

Grades *are* important for college entry, for participating in sports or other extracurricular activities, or to enable students to avoid punishment by parents. In young lives, these are crises, and students can be very persuasive in begging teachers to support them. Perhaps you feel that there is too much emphasis on grades; you would have many supporters. Suppose you decide, "Well, just this once . . ." Don't do it!

Allegations of a single grade change can throw the integrity of a school's grading system into doubt and provide the media with weeks of stories. Everyone loses face!

MOTTO: A grade recorded accurately is forever.

Don't make diagnostic remarks on record cards.

When parents or students are allowed to review record cards, those cards must be free of *any* defamatory comments. Otherwise, the teacher who entered them may be liable for defamation of character. Of equal importance, teachers reviewing record cards in subsequent school years may be biased against students based on comments they have read that may be completely misleading, inaccurate, and certainly out of context.

Teachers *may* choose to describe behavior in these ways: "John's mother claimed he was ill often this year." "John's difficulty with other children often is the result of his poking them with sharpened pencils." "John repeatedly takes pencils and other personal items off my and other students' desks." "John had 25 unexcused absences this term."

When motives are ascribed to behavior, or value-laden terms are used—thief, kleptomaniac, psychotic, hateful, malicious, stupid, and so forth—even clinicians can be on thin legal ice. The potential for harm may be greater than the necessity for notation.

Furthermore, student behavior can be precipitated by transitory situations in the home that no longer exist in future months or years. When behavioral notations are made, usually there is no follow-up or closure to the original entry, and readers may assume the behavior continues unabated. With special education students, special care is required. Behavioral notations should be limited to those made by certificated staff members.

A child who is happy and quick to laugh usually isn't labeled manic. Likewise, a child who isn't outgoing or who appears sad shouldn't be labeled depressed. Labeling leads to "hardening of the categories." Think carefully before writing, "He is . . ."

MOTTO: Misdiagnosis can be hurtful and costly.

Report suspected drug use immediately.

❧❧❧

Drug use is so pervasive that even elementary school staff must be observant for indications of drugs on campus. Classroom teachers are potentially among the best observers of changed behavior among students or of unusual paraphernalia in purses or book bags. Teachers must overcome the reluctance to see and pay attention to bleary eyes, slurred speech, unexpected and continuing fatigue. Behavior communicates—but who's to hear and see if teachers choose not to do so? Really, teachers must.

Sometimes, snatches of conversations are overheard. Sometimes, students provide clues for teachers to observe specific individuals. Hangovers, nervousness, appearance of being strung out are hard to miss. What to do? First, talk with students. Ask for information: "Is something wrong?" "Are you not well?" "Is your usual good mood taking the day off?" Any help you can provide begins with a question.

Next, you record your observations and actions *as specified by school policies.* You may also ask your school nurse or counselor to consider intervening or, given your relationship with parents, call them to *discuss the behavior you observed* and ask for their input or at-home support. Again, refer to your school policies, and follow them.

If a student is willing to talk about drug use, it is not sufficient to extract a promise to quit. A lot of clinical and criminal data document the requirement for specific assistance. Professional help is needed to guide students toward wellness. They cannot do it alone, and you may be the first and best means of defending the student's future from the trap of drugs and academic and athletic defeat. If not you, then who?

❧❧❧

MOTTO: Reach out and stop someone.

Stay in your _professional_ role; keep personal details to yourself.

Your students are _not_ your friends, nor are they peers. They are impressionable young people who may see you as a model for the kind of adult they wish to become. What you tell them about your personal life—things you've done, mistakes you've made—may legitimize their taking risks because you did. If parents hear that you planted the idea, the personal and career consequences can be substantial.

Speeding tickets, nervous breakdowns, affairs, abortions, miscarriages, divorces, suicide attempts all are parts of the human experience. If you've had them, _do not share them._ By relating that you survived them and succeeded (you _are_ an authority figure!), you may provide an inappropriate role model. Although it's natural to want to comfort others by sharing your experiences, remember who you are, where you are, and what you're paid to do.

Parents want teachers to be good role models, to be guardians of the status quo, and to equip their children for advancement into a successful life. Students want teachers to care about them, be kind, be entertaining, and make it easy for them to get the information and grades needed to meet their immediate academic goals. Administrators want teachers who perform their instructional duties without creating problems. No one in these constituencies needs to discover that teachers have life histories outside their preparation to be conduits to subject matter content and expertise. Even your most mature students can become confused when teachers cross the line between role model and confidante, between subject matter expert and personal adviser, between authority figure and imperfect human being with feet of clay.

MOTTO: Be a teacher first, last, and always.

Don't be sarcastic in the classroom.

Students hear more verbal communications from their teachers than from their parents. Also, students are subject to enormous peer pressure to conform. When students hear teachers speak sarcastically or use sarcastic put-downs in responding to classmates who give incorrect answers or ask "dumb" questions, often they interpret it as an okay way to interact. In a "monkey see, monkey do" reflex, students will affect sarcasm as part of their communications pattern, and parents will not be pleased.

In one instance, a student new to the school didn't respond quickly enough when the teacher asked him a question. The teacher quipped, "Perhaps if you cleaned out your ears, you might hear me when I call on you." The boy's face reddened and he hung his head in embarrassment as the teacher moved on to another student. Later that day, the boy's mother came to the school wanting a school board reprimand for the teacher as a minimum and offering a lawsuit if that didn't happen. Why? Her son was recovering from an ear infection, using external medication, and interpreted the teacher's remarks as a critique on his cleanliness. Much ado about nothing? Not at all!

As mentioned in Savvy Secret #53, students are not peers; they are not free to return smart-mouth responses to their teachers. They are in school to learn appropriate ways to behave in middle-class society: that is, to speak clearly, carefully, and respectfully as future authority figures. The medium *is* the message. When you are not important enough to be addressed respectfully, self-esteem takes a hit! When teachers hit students verbally, the "less than" messages can result in lowered performance and expectations.

**MOTTO: Leave the hurting puns outside the classroom—
they're a low form of humor.**

Think carefully about your awards and rewards.

Motivation continues to be an intriguing concept. How do you condition students to learn, to perform chores, to do homework, to break inappropriate habits, to acquire new habits, and to exhibit good citizenship in the classroom? Classic behavior modification theory advises rewarding approximations of the behavior you want, thereby moving students progressively from where they are at the outset to what you want them to be.

Remember gold stars on your forehead? If everyone gets them, how can you feel special? Or the time a student's work was praised so extravagantly that you and your classmates felt totally demotivated, incapable of competing? Motivation can be tricky.

Children like candy. Why not give candy as a reward? In small, individually wrapped pieces, candy is easy to handle and affordable. But what about the child who's diabetic or on a medically supervised diet? What about gift certificates for a hamburger and fries? Would that be appropriate for the student who comes from a vegetarian home? What can you offer that would be appropriate incentives for all students?

Review Savvy Secret #39 regarding gifts. Write down the reasons you want to provide tangible rewards and awards. Then, write down some gift ideas (a) that are age and subject matter appropriate, (b) that children will appreciate, (c) that you can afford and (d) what the criteria are for receiving them. When you decide, send a note to parents explaining your incentive system, the gifts you will use, and the criteria students will have to meet to be eligible for awards, and ask for their input regarding restrictions plus their signed permission for their child to participate. Keep those signed responses. Ditto for late admissions.

MOTTO: Rewarded effort is remembered and repeated.

Don't make student appointments away from school.

Although books on management and negotiation may recommend having problem-solving meetings on neutral turf, it's not a good idea for teachers trying to achieve problem resolution with students. School business should be conducted on school property.

A natural temptation is to meet students where they will be comfortable—a fast food place or a park. Resist it. What do teachers and students have to discuss that requires that kind of neutral space? If the subject is so "hot," the teacher should call on professional resources from the school district; if the subject is not, there's no reason for teachers to put themselves at risk by meeting students—any students—in any nonschool setting except at officially sanctioned events. Even then, teachers should be with groups of students unless they are in a coaching situation in which one-on-one contact is usual and expected. If this sounds restrictive, it is and intentionally so.

It's important to get to know students, to give them a chance to talk about problems, and to give the teacher an opportunity to promote special opportunities for scholastic or athletic advancement. This can be done in a quiet corner of the classroom while other students are busy or with the classroom door open, during a walk on school grounds while other students are present but not within hearing, or during a *scheduled* home visit when at least one parent is present. These settings should not create jealousy among other students who are not getting the same attention or set tongues wagging about motives or propriety. If propriety becomes an issue, both the student and the teacher can be harmed, and it will require administrative intervention. No one wins.

MOTTO: Be cool—make it a rule to meet at school.

SAVVY SECRET #57:

Never transport students in your personal car.

This is an extension of the logic presented in Savvy Secret #56. It is intended to be restrictive and to protect teachers against submitting to compassionate impulses that have a high probability of being misinterpreted and leading to personal and career damage.

You're leaving school. There's little Billy standing by the front door. He's been sneezing and looking ill all day. It's raining. His mother is late in picking him up. You speak to him, and he is shivering. You touch his forehead, and he seems to have a fever. Why not put him in your car and take him home?

Because: (a) His mother may arrive moments later, frantic because little Billy isn't where he is supposed to be. (b) The mother goes to the principal's office in hysterics and causes a "Where is my child?" flap. (c) Little Billy gets sicker; maybe he passes out, and you're alone with an unconscious child. (d) Or because it's raining and the streets are slick, someone slides into you, and little Billy is injured. (e) Or maybe you have engine trouble or a flat tire. (f) Or maybe little Billy, in his delirium (or as an act of malice), accuses you of touching him in inappropriate ways. (g) You arrive at his home, and no one is there. (h) Unknown to you, police are looking for little Billy's kidnappers. (i) The mother, with lawyer, reporters, and video cameras in tow, declares she's going to sue the school district, the principal, and you. Implausible? Not at all!

Think! Override your first impulse to respond as a warm and caring surrogate parent and cause the system to work for you and the student. It's a rare instance in which precipitous action is required. Think! Ask for help. Inform your administrators.

**MOTTO: The system is there to
support you and your students—use it!**

Use students' proper names.

Our names are important. Each person's name is like an ID badge. We respond when we hear our names called and, subconsciously, we listen for them to be called. When we meet others with the same name, we look at them carefully for other similarities. We may wonder why we were saddled with our given names but, however it came about, they belong to us and we to them. To hear someone use our names incorrectly is painful. To have someone minimize the significance of our names is infuriating. That's why police are schooled to speak to detainees with respect, to say Sir and Ma'am. Research has proved that displays of respect minimize the risk of physical assault.

In other years, students with "foreign" names often were given replacement identities by teachers, anglicized names that were in common usage. It's surprising how many adults still are resentful that no one could bother to learn their names.

Today's ethnic sensitivity and awareness arose as the myth of the melting pot gave way to ethnocentrism and a proliferation of names that don't fit middle-class nomenclature. Teachers must be careful to master names, no matter how many syllables and subtle intonations are required. Self-respect and self-esteem are not the most important elements in education, but the teacher who diminishes these in the eyes of students does great damage. Frequently, children can feel "less than" and reduce their efforts to learn when they feel disparaged by something so simple—and so obvious—as feeling too unimportant for their teachers to learn their names. My name is . . . !

MOTTO: A rose by any other name
would *not* be so sweet!

It's the principle—principal—of the thing.

A ship without a rudder, a car without a steering wheel, a restaurant without a chef—you get the picture. Things get out of control. Every organization needs a leader, someone whose responsibility is not only to control but to facilitate professional freedoms for contributors. In industry, that's the boss. In school, that's the principal.

To survive and succeed as a teacher, support your principal. To support your principal, look at the school and the entire faculty as dynamic and interdependent. When the "machine" doesn't work correctly, students suffer first. Then, it's the teachers' turn. Among your colleagues are those afflicted with procedural myopia; that is, any announced procedure is viewed as a reduction of teacher prerogatives. That makes the principal a villain and teachers the victims. Teachers who buy into such negative interpretations will be unhappy; their unhappiness will be communicated to students, parents, and administrators; and they will be looking for a new job next summer.

If you feel aggrieved by something your principal says or does, think it through. What is the issue, the essence of your discomfort? When you have that clearly in mind, ask for an appointment to discuss your perception and the questions you have. In the process, keep your queries to yourself. Don't field test your responses with others in the teachers' lounge. As soon as you tell another, your secret is out. Likewise, if there's a clique whose members constantly berate the principal, find someone else with whom to share lunches and coffee. And don't repeat what you hear! At some later date, it won't matter that you didn't originate the defamatory material. It came out of your mouth!

MOTTO: Follow the leader is more than a game—it's the principle that matters.

SAVVY SECRET #60:

Know who's who and who does what.

Without a program, you don't know who the players are—whether you're in a stadium or a theater. Sometimes, you have to create your own "program," a tabulation of names, roles, and functions, so you can understand how business is done in your school.

When you're new in a school, ask for a personnel directory for the school and the district. Discover what kinds of support personnel are available to support you and your students. Discover where they're based and how to get in touch with them. Are counselors on staff in-house or do they visit and how often? Is there a school nurse, and what hours is he or she available?

When do you contact the attendance officer, and how do reach him or her? Who heads up your school's custodial staff? Who's the school's dietitian? Is there a gang coordinator, conflict resolution coordinator, job placement staff, driver training staff?

Who is your in-school union representative and the district president? Most of all, who is your school's secretary, and what have you done to become his or her friend?

This is not a recommendation to enlarge your circle of friends. Each of these professionals—and others not mentioned—is on staff to support school district programs, which, ultimately, means students and teachers. Each has expertise, and you need to know when and how to access it to support your students and for your peace of mind. Peace of mind? If an episode with a student results in litigation in which you are named, it will be to your benefit to have records that show that you sought help from appropriate in-school or district support staff. Don't delay. Find out who's who.

MOTTO: You don't have to do it alone.

SAVVY SECRET #61:

Do it by the book.

Many teachers have agonized over this question: Because learning is such an individual process, how can it be successful in an environment governed by rigid rules and policies? Some teachers are so turned off by school district bureaucracies that they refuse to read their district's policy manual and personnel manual. Principals and other administrators confirm this. They say that many of the problems that involve litigation and dreadful public relations result when teachers do not follow procedures outlined in manuals they have been given. The truth is, no teacher is professional who ignores the policies and procedures developed over time by school districts in response to recurring problems.

Rather like the procedures for safe vehicle operation mandated by your state's department of motor vehicles, which are based on accident prevention research, school district policies and procedures are *your professional rules of the road*. Learn them to a point of easy familiarity—that is, you can find the reference to answer any question you have, almost instantly. If you find the manual(s) to be unclear on a point that's important to you, check it out with your department chair, principal, or union representative. But do so respectfully, in a manner that says you want to learn and not to prosecute. The point you raise may be about a restriction that no one likes but that everyone follows. Petulance on your part will mark you as a potential problem teacher.

This recommendation—advice!—is buried in the middle of this book, because it *is* an unpopular subject. Many teachers respond to "by the book" the way heavy people respond when asked, "How many calories are in that piece of pie?" No one likes that.

**MOTTO: Teachers who follow rules
contribute to successful schools.**

SAVVY SECRET #62:

Get it in writing!

This is a recurring theme (see Savvy Secrets #7 and #20). These *are* litigious times, and teachers are members of a vulnerable profession. For example, your class is interrupted by a man who claims to be Mary's uncle. He says Mary's mother has been taken to a hospital, and he was asked to pick Mary up. Mary says the man is her mother's brother and goes to stand by his side. Do you let them leave? No way! Not until you have sent a note to the principal with the uncle's request and that note has been returned with the principal's signature. Will it be an aggravation for the principal? Quite the contrary.

Principals get into hot water with district administrators any time a teacher's actions are questioned. When you require an authorizing signature, you protect your principal as well as your career. It's an old saying, but—Better safe than sorry!

Even if you have written permission from parents or guardians and a situation comes up that sets off your mental fire alarm, confirm the action requested with your principal or some other administrator. Don't go against your own gut feelings.

Nearly half the children you teach come from homes in which one or both parents have been divorced. That multiplies the number of people who can claim to be relatives, and whose relationship may be verified by a child, but who should not be allowed to remove a child from school—and from your protection. Pay attention!

Child release is specified here, but there are other things teachers can be asked to do that can put the unwary into jeopardy. There are too many to cover here, but they will be specified in your policy manual. Think of it as your career first-aid manual.

MOTTO: You're in charge, so stay in charge—
and protect yourself, too.

Don't use physical exercise as punishment.

Maybe you remember the coach who used to say things like, "Okay, smart mouth, let me have 50 push-ups." Then he would have everyone else stand in a circle and count the push-ups, laughing while the miscreant sweated them out. Some coaches like to believe this builds character or strength. But really, it's abuse of role.

Many complain that students lack discipline. Probably, what they mean is that students often lack a desire to learn. When punishment is used in classrooms and on playgrounds or athletic fields, it tends to invoke resistance and avoidance rather than creating scholastic focus. Punishment is a powerful and recurring theme in American culture. It's the shortcut to short-term compliance. In the long term, it tends to be counterproductive. So far, research has not been able to overcome the impulse—even among the gentlest teachers—toward retaliation and revenge when students step out of line, violate a rule, or release pent-up energy in an angry outburst.

A major by-product of education is socialization, which, in large part, is a function of self-discipline. Self-discipline is learned behavior, best taught by demonstrations of appropriate behaviors. When teachers structure educational situations, they demonstrate the exciting progression of learning and skill acquisition. Then, by allowing students to participate in creating classroom rules, procedures, and consequences, they demonstrate self-discipline in action. Physical punishment is contrary to all this and shuts down the spirit of inquiry that drives learning processes. Physical punishment is prohibited by many districts. Make sure you know how it's defined in your district, and comply!

MOTTO: Discipline works best from inside out.

Don't stay late after school.

Ɛ✺Ɔᴖ

In other times, teachers used the quiet hour after school to mark papers, to put up (or take down) decorations, to speak to a special student, or to plan the next day's activities. Now, given the security problems that plague so many schools, it's unwise for teachers to remain in empty classrooms—even at lunch time. A teacher alone can become an easy mark for an intruder. It's an unpleasant thought but necessary. Be forewarned.

Even years ago, a teacher working late in her classroom was asked by the custodian not to do that any more. He said he couldn't complete his tasks because it was necessary that he stay near her classroom to guard her! These are some ugly realities.

As for staying late to visit with students, flash back to Savvy Secret #44 and review the reasons for not doing that. If you must have a special chat with a student, ask to use the office of the nurse, the counselor, or the principal. Such offices provide the security of having someone else know what you're doing, plus you have the opportunity for privacy, if that's required. (As recommended before, ask for an office with inside glass walls or door panels.) Such meetings and the subject discussed should be noted in your calendar or lesson plan, though notes about the conversation need not be kept. The important point is to ensure there's no doubt about your purpose and agenda.

An alternative, but not one that's highly recommended, is for teachers to team up if they have to stay late, perhaps taking turns being in the other's classroom while necessary chores are performed. An inconvenience, to be sure, but smart. Thinking ahead and asking for help can prevent a lot of long-term, unpleasant consequences.

MOTTO: When it's time to go, go!

Don't initiate self-esteem or value-construct programs.

Following up on Savvy Secret #16, there's agreement that it's desirable for students to have high self-esteem and to develop an ethical system based on values accepted by parents and the community at large. Educational professionals know that low self-esteem, based on things that happen outside the school, compromises the abilities of many students to learn. That raises this question for some educators and many parents: Should schools provide training in belief systems, or is that done better by families and religious groups?

It has not been too many years since driver education was widely and actively opposed by community groups; only massive campaigns by insurance companies and police agencies were able to overcome the resistance by presenting powerful economic and casualty data. So far, there's no research base and few community groups who will fight for values-construct training in classrooms that opponents believe should be focused entirely on academic pursuits. And, given the variety of the antivalues groups and their access to media, it would be a foolish teacher who invites them to challenge his or her choice of curriculum content. Let those decisions be made at the district level!

Still, if your district has included a self-esteem or values program in the district's curriculum, it's a good idea to notify parents in advance about the program, its content, and the issues it will address, and invite them to discuss program content. Should any parents be opposed to the program or content, arrangements can be made *in advance* to have their children excused from those lessons. That way, if parents complain, you have taken a major step toward elevating conversations to a constructive level.

**MOTTO: Before you jump on
the bandwagon, make sure it's there.**

Be sensitive about book assignments.

Because books and reading are so intricately entwined with today's curricula, care must be taken by teachers when making reading assignments. Of course, you will use in your classroom only those books that have been approved. To do otherwise invites hazard. In fact, it's a good idea to send parents a list of the books you plan to use each semester, with annotations that explain why the books were chosen and which approved lists they're from. Then, parents have an opportunity to prescreen what their child will read and to return any comments or reservations.

R. L. Stine has sold a great many books (*The Goosebump Series*). From the sales, one might infer that children like to be frightened and that parents know their children like books in the series because they keep buying them, and the sale of tee shirts, hats, and other Goosebump products suggests that children identify with the characters. On the other hand, some children do not enjoy being frightened, and some parents do not approve of scary content in reading material.

If a child recently has lost a parent, a book about death and dying may be very upsetting. (Some children even find that perennial favorite, *Charlotte's Web*, upsetting.)

At the high school level, where there is concern about teenage suicide, even the classic *Romeo and Juliet* comes under fire. So-called age-appropriate books may not be, given the emotional development of the student, and that's the kind of sensitivity teachers need to employ. It's another level of concern and another disagreeable reality. But students deserve your sensitivity. Parents demand it. Give it to them.

MOTTO: Books are tangible evidence of classroom teaching.
Don't surprise parents.

Don't allow profanity in your classroom.

U.S. English seems awash in four-letter words. TV and movies, targeted at the adolescent market, pander to the lowest common denominator in communicative skills. Perhaps there's no verbal child in the United States whose vocabulary doesn't include formerly forbidden words. Worse, if TV portrayals truly are representative of U.S. life, "bad" language is as much a staple of the U.S. household as cold cereal and milk.

Make your classroom a "neutral territory" in which profanity and obscenity are not allowed. Although it may not be true that using profanity is the sign of a limited vocabulary, it is a sign of diminished respect for the institution within which it's used.

One teacher, trying to encourage students to be creative while following the introduction-body-conclusion structure in their essays, chose not to censor unfortunate word choices. Soon, students interpreted toleration as advocacy, and essays became contests among students to see how far the teacher's tolerance would extend. The essays soon were circulated, profanity began to pop up in other classes, parents learned of the game, and the principal had to step in to protect the teacher from her folly.

There is an overriding reality in schools: They are public institutions. As such, they must not veer too far from community norms (or what involved parents and political leaders claim are normative values). Any behavior exhibited by students that's outside the norm will be blamed on the schools by someone, and that means heat for the administration. Make sure the spark can't be tracked to your classroom. Better to be known as the school prude rather than the prince or princess of crude.

**MOTTO: I've heard it before,
but I don't want to hear it here.**

SAVVY SECRET #68:

Get reports and other paperwork in on time (or early).

⟨⦿⟩

One of the universal elements of organizational life—in any organization—is paperwork and weekly, monthly, quarterly reports. Schools are no different. Only the kinds of reports may be different. Another universal element is frustration with procrastinators, the people who fail to realize that their reports are necessary so aggregate reports can be collected, collated, tabulated, and submitted. If you are a procrastinator, if your reports frequently are late, if your department chair or principal has to hound you for reports, this Savvy Secret's for you! Pay attention, because what follows can save you grief.

Get organized. Most reports are repetitive, same time each period. Most meeting or special event reports are due within a week. Plan books must be submitted each week. Special projects usually are scheduled well in advance. Anecdotal records can be compiled quickly from brief entries in your daily calendar. As the athletic shoe people say, "Just do it!" Daily. As the time management experts say, "First things first, secondary things next, tertiary things whenever." Yes, the *primary* job is teaching, but teachers' salaries, book supplies, and administrative support are based on numbers, the statistics that come from the bottom up. They begin at *your* level, and everyone in the system is dependent on you to get your data in—accurately and on time.

If you need additional structure, here's a way to create it: Don't go to bed Friday night until paperwork due on Monday is done. Then, you can enjoy your weekend. During the week, get the next day's paperwork done before dinner. Then, you can enjoy your evening. And so on. This is easy. What's difficult is Why? Truly, no one cares why!

MOTTO: A major bureaucratic sin is failing to get paperwork in. A stitch in time. . . .

Don't speak or act in anger; it comes back to haunt you.

Expressing authentic feelings is important. Being upset or frustrated is legitimate. Being angry *rarely* is. Getting angry in the classroom never is. The magic word is *control*—get in control, stay in control, and don't lose control, especially of yourself. When you lose control—get angry—you say things that can't be retracted and behave in ways that can destroy your effectiveness as a positive, rational, adult role model.

Some teachers seem to feel that anger is a reality, a part of life that kids have to learn to deal with. "When I'm angry," they say, "the kids know it, and they're just going to have to deal with it." Angry outbursts by adults toward children is called verbal abuse in some circles and emotional battery in some states. Neither is acceptable.

You cannot afford to vent, to use the classroom as a dumping ground for pent-up feelings. If you feel you're going to "lose it," call for reinforcements and get out of the classroom. *It's better to leave the scene than to cause one,* destroying relationships and marking you as an unreliable hothead. If anger is a continuing problem, get professional help. Make visual or mental cues to prompt anger control techniques. If they work for you, share them with your students. Over 5,000 peer mediation projects, in which students help each other cope with anger and rage, have produced positive results. Given the numbers of children who come from rageful environments, schools and teachers must create neutral zones where kids can be at peace and free from threats of violence that so often follow anger. Teaching and learning require peace of mind. The classroom is *not* your therapy center. Don't release your anger there.

**MOTTO: Blessed are the peacemakers,
who have put their anger behind them.**

Please, just the facts when discussing your students with authorities.

One of the tenets of psychology is that people cannot tolerate ambiguity—an incomplete picture. We need to "close the loop" by inferring a cause for every action observed. This is the machinery of gossip and often, the unintended cause of great harm to others. We are told to suspend judgment and not to be judgmental. It's an almost superhuman effort to overcome that which is so natural. Good work if you can do it!

When discussing your students, stick to the facts as *you* know them, as you heard them directly from the student, or as you observed them. Do not embellish. Do not go beyond what you saw or heard. Do not close the loop or join others in speculating about antecedent events or causes. Be particularly careful with other teachers, teaching assistants, or other support staff so you don't launch a chain of gossip.

If you are questioned by police or court authorities about a student, remember that you do *not* have to answer questions unless you are subpoenaed. Ask your principal to sit in during such interviews, or at least, discuss the situation with an administrator. If you don't have *relevant* information—knowledge that bears *directly* on the legal questions being addressed—say that. Your impressions are just that.

The rule of thumb is that anything you say will be repeated, if not attributed directly to you. Therefore, it's necessary to be careful of what you say, to have a witness or at least a tape recording of any interviews. This is a time when having written authorization from your administrator to discuss a student with a third party is particularly appropriate. Don't put yourself and your district in legal jeopardy.

MOTTO: The less said, the better— and the more easily defended.

Be careful when discussing difficult subjects with students.

A student new to the school confided to her teacher that she was afraid of male teachers because of what had happened at another school and that she had been the victim of incest. The teacher said she hoped everything at home was all right now, but the student replied that things always had been okay at home, that it was only at school that she was afraid. Confused, the teacher asked, "But the incest? Was it your father?" The student became upset and told the story at home that the teacher had accused her father of incest. After several painful days, the issue was resolved and the teacher was not rebuked. The cause? The student had misunderstood the meaning of "incest."

Teachers frequently find themselves caught between wanting to disbelieve what they hear from children and not wanting to convey to the child that he or she is not being believed. Children can exaggerate. Children can create stories for their own amusement or to get attention. Sometimes, the truth is so bizarre that it's hard to discern. That's why teachers are advised to ask *gentle, leading questions,* such as, "Do you want to tell me what happened?" or "Can you tell me more about what was going on?" or "Excuse me, I didn't understand what you just said. Could you repeat it?"

Many times, these clarifying questions will reveal that nothing is being described that constitutes a threat to the child. When you are sure of that, then the issue is one of having time just to let the child talk. If you *feel* that something inappropriate is going on, ask the school counselor or nurse to stop by, and set up the story line so the child gets to retell the story. As the teacher in the example learned, "Listen with a third ear."

MOTTO: Be sure that what you heard is what was meant.

Don't talk with children about matters under criminal investigation.

This book was written because we live in a litigious society, and educators can be involved in lawsuits that can damage them professionally and financially. Teachers and school districts are easy targets for aggrieved parents and special interest groups. This book suggests ways to stay out of the fray.

When litigation visits your school or intrudes in your life, every conversation about the case can be the basis for jeopardy. Involved students may want to share confidences with their teachers, inadvertently making their teachers participants in the litigation. What you know about, you can be compelled to testify about as a principal witness. Students get caught up in the drama and excitement of such events. If they are directly involved, they often have a need to prove themselves to be without blame among those whose respect they seek. Teachers frequently are included and are offered the "the inside scoop" in return for the teacher's absolution and continued acceptance.

If students wish to discuss a case with you, explain to them that although you care about them, you cannot discuss the case, that their information about the case should be communicated to the attorney assigned. If they persist, try to involve the school counselor (who *may* have confidentiality privileges in some districts).

Teachers must support children who are distressed and assure them they are not being judged or rejected; but you need to avoid becoming possessor of facts that could be damaging to you and the student. These twin sensitivities emphasize the boundaries between being a teacher and a friend, between being a role model and a confidante.

MOTTO: When litigation is involved, what you know can hurt you.

Don't go it alone. No organization appreciates solo players.

⋘⊙⊚⊙⋙

There is strength in unity. There is credibility where there are corroborating witnesses. When teachers act alone, administrators naturally wonder, "Why is no one else bothered by this?" However, this is *not* a recommendation to be an activist in antiadministration causes (which is a certain way to initiate an unplanned change in employment).

When you have a problem student who's continuously disruptive in class, ask the question, Who else is having trouble with him or her? Maybe it's a case of bad chemistry, and that's what you might hear if you go alone to seek administration's support. But if other teachers, school counselors and psychologists, and so forth are experiencing the same kinds of difficulties, you will get a different response from administrators.

From a practical point of view, you have only so many "chips" to play with administrators. Do your homework so you can use them well. Homework, here, means checking out your experiences and difficulties with others, asking for feedback on your perceptions, and looking for different ways or means or tools for coping and succeeding.

In the classroom, why not involve students in creating disciplinary rules and consequences? Why not teach basic democratic processes while developing a classroom code of conduct? Why not send copies home with students, asking parents for comments or calls? With students and parents involved, *you're not going it alone!*

There's a strong ethic in the United States about individual effort, about being the come-from-behind savior of the day, about saying and doing things for which others lack stomach. That's a strong model to override, but the evidence says it's worth doing.

⋘⊙⊚⊙⋙

**MOTTO: There's strength in numbers,
wisdom in numbers, and safety, too**

Don't get emotionally involved with students.

Students often are lovable. In elementary school, they can remind teachers of the children they once were, of nieces and nephews, or of long-dead child relatives. Some teachers find it difficult to avoid fixating on such students, lavishing extra attention on them that is unfair at many levels to other students. Likewise, as students emerge into young adults, full of vitality and energy (and raging hormones), teachers of both sexes can lose their emotional and professional bearings. They sometimes override everyone's advice and common sense and initiate relationships that only rarely aren't doomed to end badly, if not tragically. Few things are so damaging to the profession.

In one case, a male student misunderstood a female teacher's extra efforts to help him overcome family and academic problems. She made the mistake of meeting him off campus and in her home when her husband was absent. The boy fell in love, and though the teacher did nothing to encourage other than a teacher-student relationship, the boy's fantasies about her were verbalized to friends. Soon, there was a scandal. She had to leave teaching. Her husband, an administrator in another district, also was devastated, personally and professionally, and is looking for work outside education.

In another case, an effective male teacher, on the fast track to the top, fell in love with a female student in her junior year. He contained himself until she graduated. Then, with her parents' permission, he and the girl began dating. When his district's administration found out, he lost his department chairmanship, was removed from his school, and the only fast track that remained to him was the one out of town.

MOTTO: Don't let responses in the affective domain override your brain.

Don't waste anything—conserve!

Most experienced teachers remember years when they had to buy pencils and reams of copy paper for students along with chalk, poster paper, magic markers, crayons, and other classroom supplies. Many students continue to learn from obsolete texts held together by duct tape and attend classes in poorly maintained buildings. These circumstances say education is losing in the competition for community resources.

This creates a natural opportunity to teach students to conserve resources, including storage space. There should be a place for everything, and everything should be in its place when not in use. This is an opportunity to teach children to protect toys, books, and equipment by storing them properly and to teach basic housekeeping skills by having all participate in clean-ups and put-aways. It's an opportunity to build habits of thoughtful use of shared resources, which is fundamental to good citizenship.

Paper can be used on both sides. Pencils can be used for months if they are not chewed or broken or used inappropriately for busy work. Chairs, tables, student desks, and science equipment are expensive to buy and replace. Interesting, isn't it, that they don't wear uniformly? Equipment in some classrooms deteriorates faster than in others.

Teachers have been cited for allowing equipment to be abused. Somehow, they haven't modeled behavior appropriate for proper care of facilities and equipment, nor have they required their students to treat property with respect. Ditto with damage to doors, window sills, and carpets and consumption of electricity and water. These may seem like trivial items, but *true* conservation begins with details. Teach them!

**MOTTO: Waste not, want not—
and teach that to your students.**

Understand school politics, and don't get tripped up by them.

∼⊙⊙∽

A ll institutions are political, as are all continuing groups of adults. It's the way civilized people put forward points of view and agendas for change or for maintaining the status quo. But teachers must maintain political neutrality and nonpartisanship, down to the point that students should not be aware of a teacher's political affiliation.

"Politics," as in wearing party buttons and being an active campaigner for specific candidates, usually is prohibited on school property. Furthermore, even when schools sponsor mock elections as part of civics education, teachers must be impartial in their descriptions of national parties' and candidates' platforms. Impartiality is a major value in the effort to educate without bias. Even when teachers seek public office, they must be sure they cannot be quoted by their students as having advocated positions that parents will find objectionable. Staying with facts as presented in approved texts or mainstream news publications *usually* keeps teachers clear of controversy and complaints.

Likewise, when union or professional organizations are engaged in election campaigns, check your school and district rules for their definitions of *appropriate* ways for you to participate. In most districts, this is an old subject, and rules exist.

Where office politics are involved, get a fix on your school's recent history; find out where power is, who the key players are, what issues already have been resolved, and which are off-limits. Then, be mindful of the alliances you form, the cliques you join, and the way you use *your* influence and energy. Put another way, each teacher has just so many chips to play in the school's influence game. Play yours well.

∼⊙⊙∽

MOTTO: Political activism is an off-campus, after-hours activity.

Don't let your expectations get you down.

❦

"Good teaching often goes unrewarded" is a recurring headline in public and professional media. It's a fact that many teachers have worked diligently and creatively for years without ever receiving awards or recognition. That's a compelling reason for teachers to maintain the perspective that the most powerful rewards will come from their students.

What is good teaching? Every teacher has a definition, as do most principals and other administrators. Ultimately, "good" reduces to standards met and "poor" to standards missed. Truly, this is a blessing—unless you work in a school in which standards are never defined. When you know what the standards are, then you are empowered to set performance targets for yourself and your students. Then, you can measure progress, and progress always is a basis for *encouragement*. You can acknowledge student achievement—and your own. Accomplishment is a reason for rewarding yourself.

Institutional life is filled with surprises. Often, people are elevated into leadership positions who seemed to have missed out on basic interpersonal skill development. Or they missed the lecture on "Building an effective and supportive staff." Surely, "please" and "thank you" are expected courtesies, but don't be devastated when they are missing from your principal's management style. Instead, turn your disappointment into setting your own appointments with excellence and coaching your students to new levels of scholastic performance. They're your product; their performance is your best reward!

Encourage the development of standards in your school. They are necessary for professional excellence. Don't fear measurement against them. They are your best ally!

❦

MOTTO: Expect nothing, blame no one, and do something!

Don't be afraid to change or be the last to change.

༄༅

There's the story of Rip Van Winkle waking up after a 100-year nap to discover freeways, fast-food strip malls, and the Internet. "Where can I go to feel safe, where things will be as they always were? I know, I'll go to the schoolhouse!" He was right! Technologists say that innovations go industrywide in 2 years, but take 20 in education.

Schools are society's means of projecting community values forward. That makes schools repositories of the status quo, which is why school curriculum changes are attacked so often by conservative community groups. But changes are catching up with schools, as economic forces are driving school districts to become competitive with private schools in delivering "quality products"—students who are equipped to perform effectively in 21st-century organizations. The conservative elements within most schools decry the changes and have determined that they won't change, won't adapt.

Your career cannot advance on a platform of won'ts. Pay attention when you're exposed to new techniques and procedures during inservice training. Pay attention to the opportunity to lead others by your example in the classroom. Learn everything you can from these training sessions. Don't knock them before you try them. If you have negative thoughts about them, keep them to yourself, and don't hang out with the group that's knocking change. If a change can be adapted to your curriculum and lesson plans, try it. If a new technique offers better and quicker skill acquisition by students, try it. Document what you try, the specific ways in which new or modified procedures are applied, acceptance by students, and the results in terms of learning objectives.

༄༅

MOTTO: Enjoy the 21st century—
documented successes lead the way into the future.

Don't get on the defensive when people just want to be heard.

ເດ⊙໑ນ

What's the #1 thing that gets teachers—and entire school staffs—into trouble? A large-city administrator responded immediately: "Being on the defensive. Being too thin-skinned to discuss anything without feeling they're under attack. They create distance and division instead of listening and solving problems." Straight talk from a professional about teachers who have been programmed to respond defensively. In other conversations with administrators, they said, "If only teachers would give parents a chance to talk." "If they would listen, there wouldn't be a battle." "They don't seem to realize that when a kid's performance or behavior is at issue, parents are going to be defensive. When the teacher, too, is on the defensive, things go downhill in a hurry!"

With parents, be prepared to offer Plans A, B, and C to work things out with their children. Listen first, then explain the options and make a mutual decision. The teacher comes off as a prepared, caring professional, and the parents will be pleased.

When you are called for a conference with an administrator, don't get defensive. Prepare for a coming together of professionals to discuss more positive outcomes. You may want to bring materials that explain (*not* defend) your point of view or if you have others that should be considered, ask to be excused so you can get them or ask for a second meeting. The key thing to remember is this: Everyone wants you to succeed! No one benefits when a teacher fails or feels that he or she lost face. Remember, also, that administrators typically have more and different experiences they want to share. Let them! Expect to hear something useful and, probably, you will. He or she is not an enemy.

ເດ⊙໑ນ

MOTTO: The best defense can be listening for the positive.

Don't fail to ask for help when it's needed.

Although it's poor form to send all your discipline problems to the principal's office, there are times when the intelligent decision is to ask for help. If yours is a school without classroom phones straight to the office, talk with teachers in adjacent classrooms or across the hall about emergency signals—for the fight you can't break up, bullets or rocks through the windows, a mentally or physically ill student out of control, or an aggressive intruder. Be smart. Be safe rather than sorry. Don't discover your outer limits in the classroom, because then you're out of control, and the situation worsens.

But it's not just violence that requires help. Parents bring problems into discussions that you may wish to ask for help in solving or getting referrals for other resources that might provide appropriate support. Sometimes, a student will have a learning difficulty you can't overcome. Someone in your school district probably can provide the support you need. Ask for help. Sometimes, there's a special report to be submitted, but its requirements are foreign to you; ask for help rather than fumbling through its preparation and burning up a lot of personal time and energy. Sometimes, the smartest thing you can do is to ask for help from your support system or network. Don't hesitate, because you will have occasion to return the favor.

Legally, there are times when it will be to your benefit to have a record of help sought in support of a struggling student. Taking those steps stands you in good stead.

This is a logical extension of Savvy Secret #73 and is included for emphasis. This is the era of the team, the network, the interdependent professional. Ask for help!

MOTTO: Develop and rely on a network of resource persons.

Don't fail to brush up on your skills.

ভ৫৩৩

The changing nature of education creates both higher expectations and more constraints for teachers, and both require more skill acquisition. There's no shortage of staff development courses, mentor teachers, and other types of training to enhance teachers' skills—and most districts have money for training support. Take advantage of it.

One superintendent said,

> I feel sorry for the students of those teachers who avoid taking in-service courses. Failure to sharpen teaching skills cheats students twice—first, by getting less content per class hour and second, by working with a poor role model.

Lifelong learning is necessary in today's economy, and teachers who fail to keep up will be left behind. Worse, there are high correlations among teaching skills development and both students' scholastic performance and classroom discipline. Administrators who learn of teachers with problem classes and problem parents look first to the teachers' participation in staff development programs. If there's a weak record of participation, the teacher is on a fast track out of the district. "We can't afford to keep incompetent staff," one superintendent said. "They cost more than they contribute."

Computer literacy is the starting point for an entirely new and exciting approach to educating students of all ages. As more parents find their careers affected by computers, more homes have them, and politicians argue for getting the Internet into every classroom, teachers who are not computer literate are in trouble. One teacher said, "I'll take early retirement or early death before I'll use a computer." That's a career death wish! Stay current. Enhance your skills. Acquire new ones. Computers included.

ভ৫৩৩

**MOTTO: Knowledge is power—
and a great hedge against dismissal.**

Don't lie (misrepresent achievements) on applications.

⌘

Truth has a pervasive way of seeping to the surface. When it doesn't correlate closely with what people have alleged, embarrassing things happen. Increasingly, as data bases proliferate in both the public and private sectors, the opportunity to mislead or to fabricate employment history is narrowing. Or if an applicant tries to omit major career events, such as drunk driving convictions or other felonies, he or she is almost certain to be found out.

Most of America's teachers are government employees. Falsifying application information is lying to a government agency. Once that's discovered, it can follow for a lifetime. *DON'T DO IT.* If you have potentially damaging information that must be revealed on an application, attach explanatory documents and mention them in a cover letter so the reviewer is not surprised. Offer your availability for a personal interview to explain the circumstances. Often, that will keep your application out of the reject pile.

When a resume or curriculum vitae is thin, there's the temptation to include lists of courses and inservice training events. That's appropriate if you actually attended them. Again, almost everything we do goes into a data base, along with everything we claim to know or know how to do. Sometimes, cross-checks of data bases searching for staff members to be considered for specific assignments turn up a "does not match" response that leads to further cross-checks and then to embarrassment, termination, and career jeopardy. Lying on official documents is indefensible and, in most cases, inexcusable because the hiring authority has no choice other than termination. As we all have been told since we were children, always tell the truth, because truth tells.

⌘

MOTTO: Don't risk the game by signing your name to bogus data.

Don't forget to monitor your seating arrangements.

ം⊙⊙

It's been said that seating arrangements require as much skill as flower arrangement. Seating arrangements are important at parties, at professional banquets, and in classrooms. In the first two instances, seating is arranged to foster relationship building, but in the latter instance, it tends to segregate the bright students from the dull.

To be fair, human nature drives us to put the most positive and most pleasing people near us and to make distance from those who annoy us or whom we dislike. Being human, teachers can tend to do this, too. Researchers found that most classroom layouts haven't changed for a hundred years—teacher's desk at the front of the room facing rows of student desks. They observed that most of student participation comes from the front rows and down the center aisle—a classic T formation.

Another study shows that when all-boy rows or tables and all-girl rows or tables are used, teachers spend the majority of their time with the boys, sometimes almost ignoring the girls. Still other studies confirm what human nature predicts—that teachers spend more time with high-ability students rather than low-ability students. Students know this, and the less capable cluster at the back of the room. Parents know this, too, remembering schoolrooms and being acutely aware of their children's abilities. Don't let yourself be charged with favoritism. Many parents are aware of seating studies, too.

Some strategies: Rotate seating each month. Assign seats to support teams doing project work. Work from both ends of the classroom. Allow students to arrange seating. Place your desk in the middle of the room. Or the back of the room.

ം⊙⊙

MOTTO: When the music stops,
be sure everyone has a good seat.

Never use real names in your stories.

Storytelling is an ancient art and the earliest form of education. Characters made real by storytellers keep teaching for the rest of one's life. Classroom teachers use stories frequently to create analogies between current challenges and those mastered in the past by other students. In these stories, the past graduate is often the main character.

When telling these stories about students of the recent as well as the distant past, it's prudent to change names to protect the identity of stories' subjects. It's surprising how often a relative or neighbor of the subject will be in your class. Or one of your students will go home and repeat the story to parents who are friends of the former student or his or her family, who may be offended to hear of the retelling and call you or your principal. Sound farfetched? It happens often enough to merit a warning in this book.

If the central person in a story is a celebrity whose life is in the public domain anyway, then the story will have that special cachet of getting some "inside scoop" about a famous person. Otherwise, use the old device for anonymity, "Let's call him Tom."

When you tell Tom's story, be mindful that the circumstances themselves don't identify the actual person, as may happen if there is notoriety involved. People tend to remember distasteful episodes—child abuse, rape, murder, drugs—with great clarity.

The classic "example" story follows this format: sin, suffering, repentance, and redemption. The troublemaker creates a mess of his or her life, suffers the consequences, is filled with remorse and, through some act of redemptive will, regains the good graces of the community. That makes a good (and motivating!) story—with disguised identities.

**MOTTO: Don't inflict harm a second time
by using your example's real name.**

Be a good manager of classroom resource people.

In response to the public concern about reducing class sizes, many districts have begun to provide teachers' aides (by a variety of names). It takes a special person to be an aide.

An aide can be a teacher's right arm. They can be public relations supporters for you with the community. They can assist in instructional and recreational activities. They can help with discipline and coaching. They can help with classroom chores.

But . . . "they can help" does not mean they are to be relegated to housekeeping, or in anyway treated as "less than." Using an aide effectively means that a partnership exists, and effective partnerships require clarity about roles and duties, about obligations and responsibilities. *You* are the classroom manager. Having an aide allows you to have more than one supervised activity going on at the same time. This should be done by plan, and the aide should be allowed to participate in the planning.

You are responsible for the classroom and for everything that happens in it. You cannot delegate that, but you can ask your aide (who likely has lots of life experience) for input on ways to cover subject matter, how to organize work and study groups, and ways the two of you can work most effectively.

What are the aide's skills and preferences? What does he or she do well and like to do? What does district policy say about aides and how to use them? Both of you should read the policy and discuss it to ensure that you understand it the same way. Whatever you do, *don't give orders!* "Please" and "Thank You!" are powerful words. Use them often. It's surprising how far appreciation goes to motivate people who work with you.

MOTTO: The best manager is the one who lets others love their work, too.

Watch the content
of computer game selections.

Beyond the violence and explosions that have seemed to be the main staple of computer games, some are overtly sexist and racist. A suit seeking unspecified damages was filed against an Arizona school district and an educational software company in August 1996. The suit, filed by parents, alleges that their son was humiliated by classmates while playing a game called "Freedom" and that his civil rights were violated.

According to the August 27, 1995, *New York Times* article, "School's Computer Game on Slavery Prompts Suit" (p. A10), players start off as illiterate and are referred to as "boy" while they try to gain educational skills necessary to move North. "The suit contends that one character, Grandfather Cato, has lines written on the computer screen like this: 'I sees a runnin' look in yo' eyes chile. How c'n I help.'" After the lawsuit and complaints from others, the game was deleted from school district computers. The moral? Even educational corporations can make poor judgment calls.

As this example illustrates, it's necessary to screen any computer games you plan to use for instructional purposes and to review them with your antennae set for anything that could be perceived as politically incorrect. In fact, it's not a bad idea to ask for parent involvement in screening them or to form a committee of students and parents from several classes in which the games will be used. As always, be clear about the learning points you want to reinforce with the game. Don't be seduced by technology.

Also, if students are permitted to bring games into the classroom for use during free time, you could be sued for allowing other children to be exposed to objectionable material because you are supposed to oversee *everything* that happens in your classroom.

MOTTO: Don't be a mouse when it comes to computer games.

Report all threats
to administrators and parents.

ecⓈⓄⓄⱽ

Following the Savvy Secret about computer games in which action figures are bombed or zapped hundreds of times in each game, not to mention action shows on TV, children learn early about violence and how it's perpetrated. Consider this example: Two third-grade boys are fighting in the schoolyard. You separate them. One announces, "I'm going to kill you, Robbie. Watch out, 'cause you won't know when. I know where to get a gun, and I'm going to kill you!" Preadolescent bravado? Or the real thing? With the ready availability of guns and the gun-related tragedies involving kids in elementary grades, these kinds of threats cannot be ignored, nor can threats be tolerated in your school.

You do not escalate the problem by speaking with parents. You may protect a child from harm; you may protect another from doing grievous harm with legal and lifelong implications. You send a clear message to students and parents that threats are not permitted and that school is for learning and practicing the codes of civil behavior.

Likewise, if you hear a minor threaten harm to another teacher, an administrator, or parents, you must inform those people for their protection and your peace of mind.

Angry students need help. Brush up on techniques for calming upset or out-of-control students. Involve counselors and other student-support resources. Treat anger and outbursts as signals for help, and don't shrink from the task. Remember, in your classroom, what you tolerate, you validate! Who determines what's okay and what isn't? Who's responsible for maintaining the learning environment for *all* students and for student welfare during school hours? Stop the threats before they disrupt a lot of lives.

ecⓈⓄⓄⱽ

MOTTO: Don't fail to inform if threats are made.

Be protective and supportive of homeless students.

Students usually are assigned to schools near their homes but based on proof of residency. However, students from other districts may be attending your school rather than one in their home districts. To be legal, this requires an interdistrict transfer, the permission of both districts, or a decision by the county board of education. Such transfers can be made for a number of reasons consistent with enhancing a child's education and welfare. Some are parent-employment-related transfers so students can attend school near the parent's work.

For homeless students, things are handled a little differently.

Homeless students may be enrolled in your school because it is near the shelter that is a temporary home or because yours is the school they attended most recently. What matters is that you act as a buffer for them as much as possible, being sensitive particularly about home-based assignments or other activities that depend on a residence. For example, public libraries and after-school sites can serve as homework and research centers, but kitchens for experimenting or baking may be unavailable.

The most important administrative issue you must handle is getting an emergency phone number—in the shelter, a convenience store, or some other place—through which parents can be contacted.

Increasingly, there will be "special cases" requiring teachers to be flexible. But make sure you know your district's policies before you flex too far. Being homeless can be a very difficult time for students. Use your skills to minimize their pain.

MOTTO: Home is where the heart is. Have one!

Do not interfere with police on the campus.

Generally, police and administrators make efforts not to interfere with classroom activities. However, that protocol has been know to slip. Understand that police officers (and others on court-appointed business) have a right to be on campus and in the school. They can question children, put them in hand restraints, and take them into custody. One teacher felt that handcuffing a student would have been too traumatic and tried to interfere. She was given a citation for obstruction of justice! (In most jurisdictions, detainees must be handcuffed during transport for safety reasons.)

If a student is taken into custody, the school must inform the parents. If the student was taken from your class, you may want to ensure that notification happened.

You do not need to inform parents if a child is questioned, but it would seem the courteous and responsible thing to do.

If a student is questioned on campus, he or she generally has the right to have an adult of his or her choosing present. If you are asked, you do not have to accept; just be as kind and supportive as possible while recommending someone else. But if you do attend the questioning, here are two Savvy Secrets: First, do not interfere in the questioning, and do not offer information unless you are asked a direct question. Second, remember that what you see and hear is confidential. Beyond that, be supportive by your presence.

Police actions should support the goals of your community. If you feel that's not the case, confer with your principal and follow recommended complaint procedures. In the process, don't inflame your students or otherwise present a poor role model.

MOTTO: Be professional; know the law and respond appropriately.

SAVVY SECRET #90:

Get name change consents recorded.

ecoGov

Names are important, both on personal and legal levels. Earlier Savvy Secrets have discussed nicknames, ethnicity, and name pronunciation. The emphasis has been on being more formal in name use rather than less, on being careful to learn and pronounce names as an expression of respect for students. Here, the emphasis is on making sure you know what a student's name is and making certain that changes are properly recorded.

Surnames change as parents divorce and remarry; as children are adopted; and, not infrequently, as divorced women reclaim their maiden names. Given names can change, too, but more as a matter of whimsy. In all of these instances, teachers cannot oppose name changes. People—adults and students alike—can call themselves by any names they choose. With the biological parents' permission, children can assume the surname of a new stepparent. But no name change is legal until a court says it is.

However, as far as school records go, every student has one "real" name, one legal name, and all subsequent names are listed as aliases, AKA (also known as) names. That means teachers should not let parentally requested name changes lead them to forget the name of record so the student's records are maintained as required by law.

The case is often cited of the immigrant parents who were so excited about becoming United States residents that they wanted to make an all-American gesture. So they named their son John Wayne. By the time the boy got to school, his name caused much chagrin. His parents moved quickly to have his name changed.

What's in a name? All that's possible for a person to achieve—and record.

ecoGov

MOTTO: Name, please? Does it please?

AIDS watch.

Schools have long been clearing houses to ensure that U.S. children receive medically mandated inoculations. The virtual disappearance of many diseases could not have happened without the public schools having identified all of America's children and making them accessible for vaccinations. This system of checks and cross-checks is part of the schools' concerns about health education of children and health of school staff.

AIDS (autoimmune deficiency syndrome) has stumped the medical experts so far. They know how it's caused (an exchange of body fluids or dirty needles) but not how to cure it. Because of its initial identification as a disease of life-style choices, it was politicized in ways that make it difficult to discuss in schools. Several decades back, children were isolated when ill. Children with mumps, measles, and other communicable diseases were confined to their homes, which were identified when health department officials posted "Quarantined" signs by the front door. That practice has disappeared, and students with AIDS must not be isolated or prevented from participating in the full range of school activities. Having AIDS does not abridge one's right to confidentiality. Teachers must protect infected children from additional emotional pain and humiliation.

You should be motivated to teach and practice effective classroom hygiene, which provides students with habit-building opportunities. You will have guidance. Every school district should have an AIDS policy. (If yours doesn't, a model policy can be obtained from the National School Nurse's Association.) Study your district's AIDS policy and get a personal copy. Protect yourself from litigation, and protect your students.

MOTTO: Know the rules so you don't break the rules.

Understand sexual harassment, and think before you speak or act.

Most of the Savvy Secrets, the "thou shalt not" proscriptions in this book, wouldn't have been needed two decades ago, certainly not three. This one flags still other major changes in U.S. society. Court decisions and sweeping investigations have changed our male-female relationship patterns in fundamental ways. (Remember the nursery rhyme, "Georgie Porgy, pudding and pie, kissed the girls and made them cry"? Today, girls aren't supposed to have to cry over what Georgies do.)

As much as sexual harassment involves unwanted touching and attention, its most important element involves overcoming sexual stereotypes and role limitations that still are part of our culture. That makes sexual harassment a *major* public school issue and puts teachers at yet another level of risk. The most powerful antidote is a return to the formality—in word choice and tone, as well as in other behaviors—that has not been usual for a decade or more. What used to be called "liberties" among men and women (but mostly taken by men toward women) effectively are no longer defensible.

More explicit rules must be developed for conduct among students, among faculty and staff, and between staff and students. This is a useful arena for parental involvement and for study groups at all class levels. District guidelines are available. Get a copy. Read it and follow it. Be sure parents and students have copies, too.

Imagine men and women being considered equally for jobs and professions; imagine intelligence and intellect being appreciated and rewarded without respect to gender. That's what this is about. That's the destination. We've got a long way to go.

**MOTTO: It's going to be fun discovering
new ways to be men and women—together.**

Stand clear when colleagues fall in love.

Here's another area of professional hazard: romance in the workplace. For years, it's been discouraged, even forbidden, in private-sector workplaces. Recently, the prohibition has been lifted because research has indicated that companies sometimes benefit—as long as the couple are not in supervisor-subordinate relationships. This does not mean that the practice is encouraged. It isn't. If both parties are married, a lot of pain and messiness can ensue. If only one is married, that's not exactly a moral high ground. In a school setting, where teachers are supposed to be role models, such affairs (even if they lead to marriage) offer an unfortunate example of adult behavior. And if one partner is an administrator, a classic unhappy ending could be predicted.

If you encounter colleagues in a setting that suggests it isn't a business meeting and they don't see you, let them be. If they see you, act as though it's natural to see them, speak briefly, and continue on your way. When you see them next, do not mention the meeting. If they do, act as though nothing untoward occurred. Don't allow yourself to become a coconspirator. And don't repeat what you've seen, because if you blow the whistle and that makes them feel guilty or threatened, it could put *you* in a compromised position. As in detective stories, witnesses frequently become victims. In the educational food chain, teachers can be hassled or forced to resign by more senior staff who might feel threatened by your knowledge. These things—affairs between people who should know better—happen. So does retaliation toward those who know and gossip or who respond judgmentally.

MOTTO: Love can turn anyone into a fool— but please, not at school.

SAVVY SECRET #94:

Pay attention to
perks, parking, and fund raising.

Perquisites is a strange, old-world word for a military term: RHIP (rank has its privileges). One of the most certain ways for one to communicate new or outsider status is to stumble into forbidden territory. "But there were no place cards!" won't matter if you've taken the principal's *usual* seat in the faculty lunch room or the chair reserved for department chairpersons in the faculty lounge. The only thing you can do that's more damaging is to usurp another's parking place! That's a poor way to begin relationships and a certain way to get on someone's black list. Pay attention!

Remember Sociology 101? Every group has assigned or assumed roles, a pecking order, and consequences for those who don't conform to group norms (and know their place and stay in it). School faculties and staffs are not exempt from these realities.

When you're new, observe, listen, and ask questions. Be careful not to dominate discussions. Don't block three seats in the conference room—one for you and two for your coat, books, and briefcase. Smile, be kind and courteous. It will pay off.

Meanwhile, find out where it's okay to park. Until you know (or are assigned a space), avoid named or visitor spaces. Park in the most distant spaces until you know. At lunch or at meetings, until you know where it's okay to sit, wait to be invited. It's not being shy, it's being considerate of the perks others have earned. That's good politics.

And before you decide to fund a proposed student trip or classroom equipment purchases, check school and district policies! You may run afoul of prohibitions or existing fund-raising programs, creating competition with colleagues for contributions.

MOTTO: Don't sit or park where angels,
even, would fear to stop.

SAVVY SECRET #95:

Don't video or audiotape
without permission.

Even if you work in a public school, not everything that happens or is said there is in the public domain. Although taping provides immediate feedback for teachers and football players, although it provides for quick adjustments of tennis or golf swings, and although public speaking and acting classes are strengthened by taping, don't do it until you have written parental permission. It's worth the effort to avoid a firestorm of protests.

Consider this example: A kindergarten teacher used his class as subjects in a video he made for a graduate course he was taking. The lesson he developed involved his students in making sand castles, then discussing what they had learned about castle building and mixing sand and water. During the sand box sequence, one small boy was seen repeatedly moving sand with his plastic shovel. After each scoop, as he stood and turned, his shovel passed so closely over the head of a little girl that she was tapped lightly, small amounts of sand spilling into her hair. Just like "Candid Camera," the episode made the graduate students laugh, added a light moment to a graduate course, and likely contributed to the A received by the kindergarten teacher.

But guess what? One of the graduate students was a neighbor of the girl in the video. Her parents were not amused to learn that their daughter was the subject of entertainment for people outside their family. The parents demanded to see the tape, fumed that they had not given permission for their daughter to be taped or to be laughed at, and contacted an attorney. Another piece of good school work foiled by poor head work. Don't presume you have parents' permission. Don't forget it's needed.

**MOTTO: Be safe, not sorry; get permission slips
and keep them on file.**

Don't let stress creep up on you.

ⲥⲟⲟⲩ

In recent years, many teachers have taken early retirement or disability retirement because of burnout—stress. As this and the preceding 95 Savvy Secrets suggest, teaching can be a stressful profession. Here are some suggestions to prevent stress from putting you on the professional sidelines or otherwise debilitating you.

- ⟶ Exercise: Develop a regimen, and stick with it. With so much inexpensive equipment for in-home exercise available, there is no excuse for not staying in shape. Besides, rigorous exercise is known to be an effective antidote to stress and tension.

- ⟶ Socialize: Develop a circle of friends and interests beyond schools and students. Churches, civic groups, hobby groups, it doesn't matter. Do something that excites you and that you look forward to doing. It creates perspective.

- ⟶ Be diet wise: Pay attention to nutritional research and follow a diet regimen that fits your lifestyle. If you are what you eat, choose it carefully.

- ⟶ Philosophize: Yes! Read self-help books; listen to motivational tapes; find out how others overcome stress with goal setting and achievement. These philosophies are not in conflict with religious beliefs and, in conjunction, may protect against stress.

- ⟶ Fantasize: Keep an active list of things you want to do, places you want to go, movies you want to see, books you want to read, and use your self-help tools to achieve your fantasies. Dreams precede deeds. Or as the shoe people advise, "Just do it!"

Stress is real. A major part of your job—beyond competent transfer of codified data and acquisition by students—is being a role model for competent adulthood.

ⲥⲟⲟⲩ

**MOTTO: Stress and burnout are enemies
of competence. Act now.**

SAVVY SECRET #97:

Build your "brag book."

M any times in this book, you've been told to get permission slips and keep them on file. This Savvy Secret involves collecting *positive input* from parents, students, and administrators that come to you and keeping them ready to buoy you over rough spots.

- Get a notebook with plastic page protectors. When you receive thank-you notes from parents, put them in your book. Use the school's date-time stamp if you can.
- Keep your notebook current. Retrieve copies of reviews from school files; check your own files for notes from administrators or supervisory teachers. Book them.
- Keep your notebook—your brag book—safe. It can save your bacon.

How can a brag book save you? When an administrator reports that a parent has complained that you respond only to bright students, not the "average" students in your class, pull out your desk key, hold it up, and say, "Excuse me while I get my book." When you return, you might say, "Look at these notes I've received from parents of 'average' students who have appreciated my coaching them to higher grades. Why would I ignore her child?"

How? A newly promoted administrator, formerly a principal, began criticizing a teacher's classroom techniques, trying to get her to transfer to another district for budgetary reasons. The teacher got her brag book and said, "I'm surprised that you now find my methods so inadequate. Look at these reviews you gave me 2 years ago, 3 years ago, 4 years ago. How did I go from receiving compliments to criticism? Don't you find it strange?" He found another teacher—without a brag book—to accept a transfer.

The best survival tool is good performance—and a brag book to back it up!

**MOTTO: Cover your assets—
set up your reserve fund of documents.**

Postscript

೩෨෨ೲ

This primer on the new realities of classroom teaching was written with input from hundreds of current and past colleagues. It's the result of 2 years spent searching files and memories, talking with other frustrated professionals, and making the notes that were converted into these 97 Savvy Secrets. "Secrets" always must be scrutinized in context—and it's hoped you will. Do they fit in your school, your district? Which would you delete as unnecessary? Which Savvy Secrets should be included in subsequent editions? Are there anecdotes you would like to contribute? Would you like to order additional copies to give to friends or colleagues? Please write me in care of

Basics Plus
25835 Narbonne Ave., Suite 270
Lomita, CA 90717

This is a work in progress. It was conceived as a procedural "first-aid kit" for classroom teachers, one of America's most precious and underappreciated resources. As the millennium approaches, we will see a resurgence in the significance of public education and a new commitment to ensure that its promise is realized in the 21st century. Nothing is more important for our survival as a nation and our evolution as a postmodern culture of acceptance and achievement and accomplishment.

You and your peers and colleagues in the U.S.'s educational infrastructure will make it happen. But you must survive the next challenging decade. I know you will.

Recommended Reading

Adams, R., & Biddle, B. J. (1994). *Realities of teaching: Explorations with video tape*. New York: Holt, Rinehart & Winston.

Burka, J., & Yuen, L. (1990). *Procrastination: Why you do it, what to do about it*. Reading, MA: Addison-Wesley.

Drew, N. (1994). *Teaching the skills of peacemaking*. Torrance, CA: B. L. Winch.

Howard, P. (1995). *Death of common sense: How law is suffocating America*. New York: Random House.

Kriedler, W. J. (1984). *Creative conflict resolution*. Glenview, IL: Scott Foresman.

National Education Association. (1995). *Inspiring discipline*. Washington, DC: Author.

Rhode, G., Jensen, W. R., & Reaves, H. K. (1993). *The tough kid book: Practical classroom management strategies*. Longmont, CO: Sopris West.

Rist, R. C. (1970, August). Student social class and teacher expectations: The self-fulfilling prophecy in ghetto education. *Harvard Educational Review, 40*, 411-451.

Roberts, M. S. (1995). *Living without procrastination: How to stop postponing your life*. Oakland, CA: New Harbinger.

Sadker, D., & Sadker, M. (1985, October). Sexism in the classroom. *Vocational Education Journal, 60*, 30-32.

Sapadin, L., & Maguire, J. (1993). *It's about time*. New York: Viking-Penguin.

Webster-Doyle, T. (1990). *Tug of war: Peace through understanding conflict*. Middlebury, VT: Atrium.

CORWIN
PRESS

The Corwin Press logo—a raven striding across an open book—represents the happy union of courage and learning. We are a professional-level publisher of books and journals for K–12 educators, and we are committed to creating and providing resources that embody these qualities. Corwin's motto is "Success for All Learners."